American Education and Vocationalism

A DOCUMENTARY HISTORY
1870–1970

Edited, with an Introduction and Notes, by

MARVIN LAZERSON *and* W. NORTON GRUBB

CLASSICS IN

No. 48

EDUCATION

TEACHERS COLLEGE PRESS
TEACHERS COLLEGE, COLUMBIA UNIVERSITY
NEW YORK AND LONDON

TO OUR PARENTS

Foreword

The concept of vocational education, like the concept of education for life, has been a slippery one in the history of modern Western thought. Its meaning obviously depends, at least in part, on how vocation itself is defined. Some theorists—one thinks of such idealist philosophers as Johann Gottlieb Fichte or Ralph Waldo Emerson—have used the term exceedingly broadly, referring to a "vocation of man" in such a way as to make vocational education essentially inclusive of all education. Other theorists—Georg Kerschensteiner or Charles A. Prosser would be excellent examples—have used the term more narrowly, referring to a trade or craft (though never, interestingly, to a profession) for which one prepares via specific practical training. Insofar as such definitions profoundly affect the aims, the content, and the clientele of educational programs, they inevitably raise political questions; and indeed such questions have sharpened considerably in the past century, as Western society has been industrialized and Western education popularized.

It is to these relationships between vocational education and political issues that Professors Lazerson and Grubb have given their central concern in the present volume. Reflecting recent revisionist trends in American historiography, they have tried to distinguish between stated intentions and revealed preferences in vocational education programs, and between all intentions and actual outcomes. In so doing, they have argued a curious paradox about vocational education in the United States, namely, that what has traditionally been proffered as a liberal and democratic reform has often had consequences that are illiberal and undemocratic. It is an arresting argument, which sheds new light on the successes and failures of the vocational education movement.

Lawrence A. Cremin

Contents

Introduction *

In the four decades surrounding 1900, America's schools were thoroughly transformed. Fears for the socialization of the young led to a focus on family life and to new programs in early childhood education. Challenged to run their schools more efficiently and economically, schoolmen adopted business models of administration. The belief that schooling was necessary for proper moral development and economic growth accelerated the compulsory attendance movement and calls for more practical education. A society threatened by heterogeneity turned to schools for citizenship training and enlarged their social responsibilities. None of these developments were new; many simply extended, intensified, or moderately revised previous trends. Taken together, however, they radically changed the workings and functions of the educational system.

No development was more crucial to this reconstruction than vocational education. Vocationalism raised more explicitly than ever before questions about the purposes of schooling and the utility of various kinds of knowledge. It demanded that the school be closely integrated with the economy, and that the school be the

* The authors wish to thank the following for their criticism of the original manuscript: Lawrence Aaronson, Samuel Bowles, Barbara Brenzel, William Lazonick, James Medoff, Jerome Seelig, William Weber, and Janice Weiss. The research for the volume was aided by a grant from the Spencer Foundation.

primary selecting agency for the occupational structure. Questions about the criteria of selection—who should be chosen to do what—made guidance and testing fundamental to the way schools functioned. In all this, vocationalism led to a reassessment of the meaning of democracy in education.

Issues such as these lie at the heart of this book. We do not answer all the questions raised. Nor do we cover all aspects of the vocational education movement: commercial education, home economics, and agricultural education are slighted. While we mention the ramifications of vocational education—vocational guidance, educational testing, the junior high school—they are not emphasized. Instead we have chosen to focus on the development of industrial and trade education, since this aspect of vocationalism in education proved to be the primary concern of the vocational education movement during its most important phase, the years from 1900 to 1917. In the period before 1900, many of the arguments for vocationalism were developed as part of the manual training movement, and we have viewed that movement both as an entity unto itself and as a transition to vocational education. And while vocationalism has changed since 1917, most of what has happened can be best understood as a reworking and consolidation of themes and practices established during the earlier period.

MANUAL TRAINING AND THE PROBLEM
OF RELEVANCE

No American institution, wrote the journalist Richard Grant White in 1880, was "so unworthy of either confidence or pride" as the public school system.[1] Schools

---

[1] Richard Grant White, "The Public-School Failure," *North American Review*, CXXXI (1880), 537.

were condemned as centers of political corruption, marked by incompetent teachers and petty bureaucrats hostile to minimal reform. In overcrowded classrooms, dulled by the repetitiveness of recitation and drill, children studied material of ambiguous value. As criticism mounted in the 1880's and 1890's, the focus widened, ultimately including every aspect of the educational system. Yet a common demand connected the criticisms: *school and society should be integrated.* In the midst of a transformation to an urban-industrial society, Americans began asking how the school could be made more relevant to the emerging corporate industrial order.

By the mid 1880's that question was increasingly answered by the teaching of manual skills in the classroom, an issue which brought together businessmen, pedagogical reformers, technical education enthusiasts, philanthropists, and social reformers. Manufacturers demanded that schools teach basic industrial skills and sponsored machine training and industrial art. Technical educators sought to improve the practical training of engineers and future industrial leaders. Pedagogical reformers saw hand learning as part of a broader movement to invigorate classroom teaching. Those concerned about cultural standards hoped that drawing and craft instruction would restore the ideal of the skilled artisan, while social reformers turned to manual education to teach traditional moral values and bring together a disrupted industrializing society.

The movement for manual education first gained national prominence following the Philadelphia Centennial Exposition of 1876. Previously, efforts at integrating hand and intellectual learning had lacked a cohesive philosophy and had not attracted widespread attention. At the Exposition, however, a display of workshop in-

struction developed at the Moscow Imperial Technical
School raised the possibility of incorporating manual
training into all levels of schooling. Designed to teach
future engineers, draftsmen, and foremen the principles
of industrial productivity through a series of carefully
graded manual exercises, the Russian system emphasized
the separation of technical instruction from production
in direct contrast to the traditional methods of apprenticeship. In particular, the examples shown in Philadelphia influenced the two men most responsible for popu-
larizing manual education in the United States: John
D. Runkle, president of the Massachusetts Institute of
Technology, and Calvin M. Woodward, professor of
mathematics and applied mechanics at Washington
University in St. Louis.

Runkle's discovery that engineering education could
be made more practical through the teaching of manual techniques led him to establish workshops at M.I.T.,
and to begin a manual training high school affiliated
with the Institute. More important, his widely publicized reports to the Massachusetts Board of Education
contended that manual education was essential if schools
were to respond adequately to industrialism. (Doc. #1)

Runkle's views were echoed and expanded by Woodward. As Dean of Washington University's O'Fallon
Polytechnic Institute in the 1870's, Woodward had already organized workshop classes to introduce his engineering students to the use of tools. Convinced that
further shop instruction was necessary, he gained support for the establishment of The Manual Training
School at the university in 1880. Designed as a three-
year secondary school, the school combined traditional
subjects—mathematics, science, languages, history, and
English—with wood and metal work. With his school
successfully launched Woodward, like Runkle, turned to

propagandizing for manual training as essential to general education, and quickly became the movement's acknowledged leader. (Doc. #2)

Despite apparent agreement on the methods and goals of manual training, the writings and work of the movement's leading advocates contained an internal uncertainty which later served to undermine its expansion. On the one hand, Runkle and Woodward had initially applied manual training to the education of industrial leaders and professional engineers; on a lower level, they stressed the importance of their educational innovations in creating a class of skilled technicians, whose deeper understanding of complex industrial processes would allow them to supervise the machinery of American industry. The nation's demand for skilled labor would thus be met, while children of workers would be given the chance for upward mobility through education. In this respect, manual training was specifically oriented towards future vocations. On the other hand, in defending the introduction of manual training into the public schools, they were forced by the prevailing ideology of schooling as cultural education to underplay the notion that manual education trained for specific trades. Manual training educated the mind through the hand, they claimed, and was thus "as broad and liberal" as intellectual training. Emphasizing the general nature of his proposals, Woodward claimed that everyone gained from a process that taught the moral values of precision, logic, diligence, and economy.

The two leaders of the movement thus claimed they were merely balancing the excessive bookishness and abstract intellectualism of the traditional classroom with more practical learning experiences. The outcome, they predicted, would be a truly democratic system, one with greater appeal to students. "There is a wide conviction of the inutility of schooling for the great mass of children beyond the primary grades, and this conviction is not limited to any class or grade of intelligence. . . . Add the manual elements, with their freshness and variety, their delightful shop exercises, their healthy intellectual and moral atmosphere, and the living reality of their work, and *the boys will stay in school.*" (Doc. #2)

While Runkle and Woodward publicized examples of manual education, the movement drew support from leading industrialists hoping to use schools to meet their demand for skilled labor. Building upon the antebellum argument that education would further economic growth, some manufacturers contended that schools should meet specific industrial needs. A prominent example of this was industrial art, usually in the form of mechanical drawing and design, which first appeared in Massachusetts and then briefly flourished in other parts of the country. Before 1900, however, the call for public sponsorship of explicitly vocational training met widespread resistance. The manufacturers who had sponsored the movement soon withdrew, especially as it became clear that industrial art would have little effect on their industries.

Those seeking pedagogical reforms were more persistent. Their attack on the way children were taught, the rote memorization, the stultifying effects of "concert drill," the insensitivity to children's needs—all these were, and remain, a focus of sustained conflict in American education. While innovations the reformers demanded varied, the central themes remained constant: give the child material more meaningful to him and let him learn by doing. Manual training at all levels claimed to do precisely this. Drawing upon the child's natural interest in working with his hands, hand learning was an innovative and more effective way of teaching.

While the manual education movement thus had a multiplicity of themes—industrial efficiency, the preparation of skilled workers, pedagogical reform—it was tied together by several common assumptions about social change. Like most Americans of the late nineteenth century, manual training's supporters tended to idealize antebellum America as a homogeneous society in which institutions—home, workshop, church, and school—shared in the training of youth. The home taught the basic moral values and tied the generations together. The workshop and farmer's fields were adjuncts of the home; there the traditional skills and commitment to labor were passed on. For girls, the home served similar functions introducing them to the domestic ideals at the heart of stable family life. The church saw more directly to morality; the school built upon values inculcated elsewhere and advanced the child's literacy. Throughout, the assumption was of an integrated environment in which life, work, and education were inseparable.[2] (Doc. #1)

All this, manual education's proponents claimed, had changed under the impact of industrialism. Most profoundly, the relationship between man and his work had been revolutionized. Previously

the shoemaker made shoes, the carpenter built houses. Now a shoe operative repeats one process upon one given part of the shoe, and it takes about one hundred shoe operatives to make

[2] That American society had never been as stable as the imagery suggested seems to have had little effect on the rhetoric. The availability of land, labor shortages, economic and geographic mobility, and religious, ethnic, and racial conflicts had always disrupted traditional family ties, work patterns, and social class relationships.

one shoe. The carpenter may be a floor layer, a door and sash maker or a finisher, but rarely will he be a carpenter and joiner. The wage worker of today, whether a hand tool or a steam or electric tool worker, is less and less required to depend upon himself in his work. . . .[3]

Machines substituted for men, factories replaced workshops. No longer could apprentices learn skills and moral values; the master craftsman had lost his role. In the process, manual labor had become denigrated, workers were being isolated in factories, and were unable to comprehend the relationship of their jobs to the finished product. Urbanization intensified these problems. Homogeneity had given way to ethnic and social conflict. The city street had become a place of immorality, drunkenness, and crime; among the poor, family life was in disarray, a manifestation of moral failures and the lack of industrial skills.

These views that American life was being dramatically altered by industrialism created deep ambivalences. While Americans looked kindly upon the economic returns of technological growth and industrial efficiency, the social consequences were severe: urban chaos, the withering of traditional institutions, the loss of once revered values, conflict between the generations and among social classes. Indeed, the central issue of American reform in the mid and late nineteenth century lay precisely in the problem of promoting industrial growth while limiting its deleterious social effects. The school was seen as a major agent in this process. Knowledge was power, a national resource in the search for prosperity. But just as important, as a surrogate for inadequately functioning social institutions—home, workshop,

[3] Massachusetts Board of Education, *Report of the Committee Appointed to Investigate Existing Systems of Manual Training and Industrial Education* (Boston, 1893), pp. 58–68.

church—it could preserve traditional values. The battle against the slum, the muckraking journalist Jacob Riis reported, "would be fought out, in, and around the public school." [4]

Nowhere was the ideal of the school as moral agent more apparent than in the expectations for manual training; no justification for manual training was more important than the claim that hand learning would lead to individual and social reform. This idea had received its most explicit expression in antebellum activities to reform juvenile delinquents. Part of a broader movement to reform rather than punish, "houses of refuge" and reformatories for wayward youth tried to construct a therapeutic environment within which manual education was seen as a central weapon in the attack on poverty, crime, and vice. What children learned through systematic and supervised manual labor was less a vocation, however, than the moral principles inherent in hard work.

After the Civil War the ideas of the juvenile reformers became more generally applied to the social problems of industrialism. The underlying assumption, however, remained the same: social evils could be corrected by moral uplift, and manual labor was essential to inculcating morality. The problems of society, the threat of dissolution, were particularly intense in urban slums, and it was here that manual education was believed most necessary. "In tenement-house districts man-

[4] Quoted in Henry J. Perkinson, *The Imperfect Panacea: American Faith in Education, 1865–1965* (New York, 1968), p. 68. On the relationship between social reform and school reform, see Michael B. Katz, *The Irony of Early School Reform: Educational Innovation in Mid-Nineteenth Century Massachusetts* (Cambridge, 1968) and Marvin Lazerson, *Origins of the Urban School: Public Education in Massachusetts, 1870–1915* (Cambridge, 1971).

ual training is a particularly hopeful form of education," wrote social settlement worker Robert A. Woods.
"[It] is corrective and uplifting . . . Children left to
their natural impulses, provided they have the materials,
always turn to making things. Unfortunately, the boys
of this locality have few tools and little material with
which to make things. Circumstances develop their destructive side. Manual training . . . is . . . the enemy
of indifference and willfulness, because every step requires self-control, thoughtfulness, care." [5]

Woodworking, the most popular hand activity, received support as a way of integrating respect for manual labor as well as self-respect, self-reliance, and habits
of order, accuracy, and neatness. Graded exercises moved
the student from the simple to the complex, theoretically exposing him to the principles that underlay production. The moral efficacy of manual training was even
more strikingly revealed in the calls for the domestic
education of females. Girls, manual educators argued,
had once been assured of learning the value and skills
of homemaking from their mothers. Now, as had occurred with men, that condition no longer prevailed.
Especially among the poor, educators doubted that
mothers knew how or were willing to teach their
daughters the values of a moral family life, and they
quickly introduced sewing and cooking into the public
school curriculum.

While the expectation that manual training would
produce a moral reformation touched every feature of
the movement, it was most consistently applied to America's black population. Before the Civil War, manual
education for blacks had been frequently discussed in
terms of teaching skilled trades which, in an artisan

[5] Robert A. Woods, *The City Wilderness* (Boston, 1898), p. 238.

economy, would provide the free Negro with opportunities for upward mobility. After the war, black education had initially focused on literary instruction patterned after the white model and designed to show that blacks could advance intellectually. As the South moved to consolidate its racial caste system, however, manual—usually referred to as industrial—training became prominent as a special form of education for blacks. Against a background of Southern industrialism, worsening race relations, and increasing educational opportunities for whites, industrial training and Negro education became synonymous.

The movement to offer blacks a special kind of schooling was designed to provide educational opportunities within the context of second class citizenship. It assumed that education's social utility was defined by its ability to increase the individual's labor value and that the primary educational issue for blacks lay in how to instill the values of hard work in a race made indolent by slavery. These assumptions had first been articulated by Samuel Chapman Armstrong, founder of Hampton Institute in Virginia in 1868. Armstrong believed that blacks as a race were inferior, but he argued they could be made economically productive through an educational program which taught moral values through manual labor. By thus laying the basis for a stable and trained labor force, manual education would gain the approbation of white America.

While Armstrong made Hampton the first model for the manual training of blacks, it was his disciple Booker T. Washington, head of Tuskegee Normal Institute in Alabama, who best articulated and popularized the ideology of special education. Washington believed that the Negro's future lay in the South, and he therefore appealed to his race to accept social and political dis-

crimination to appease the region's white leaders. Negroes, he claimed, had to begin at the bottom and slowly
climb up the economic ladder. Social agitation served
only to antagonize whites and distract blacks from their
program of economic self-development. Recalling an
older South, Washington believed that rural life and
farming were superior to urban living and industrial
occupations, and he advocated the learning of skilled
trades, the preparation of Negroes for an artisan and
yeoman farmer class. (Doc. #3)

Washington's vision had less to do with economics
than morality, however. Like Armstrong, he blamed the
Negro for his shiftlessness and his lack of industry. The
black's problem was not political or even economic but
moral, and he needed above all else an education in
Christian character and hard work. Education at Tuskegee, Hampton, and other schools where Washington
was influential thus stressed "love of labor." The fact
that the skills learned were often irrelevant to an industrializing economy or to blacks migrating to · urban
areas was less important than the fact that such education taught honesty, persistence, thrift, and industriousness. Manual education, Washington claimed, would
turn "the downtrodden child of ignorance, shiftlessness,
and moral weakness" into "the thoroughly rounded man
of prudence, foresight, responsibility, and financial independence." [6]

Critics of Booker T. Washington, led by W. E. B.
DuBois, rejected the former's anti-intellectualism and
his subservience to Southern whites. "Negro youth,"
DuBois wrote in 1912, "are being taught the techniques
of a rapidly disappearing age of hand work." They were

[6] Booker T. Washington (ed.) , *Tuskegee and Its People* (New
York, 1906), p. 7.

not being taught the professional skills necessary for economic success in an advanced industrial economy.[7]

The economic irrelevance of manual training was only one of the criticisms which it faced, despite increasing popularity after 1880. Much of the opposition reflected an attachment to the existing curriculum and educational philosophy. William T. Harris, former Superintendent of Schools in St. Louis and U.S. Commissioner of Education between 1889 and 1906, differentiated between the higher and lower faculties, and placed manual training in the latter category. Others saw manual training as a direct challenge to the ideals of common schooling. Despite disclaimers, manual education (especially at the secondary school level) looked uncomfortably like training for trades, the channeling of public funds directly into vocational education. Manual education's roots in juvenile delinquency reform and urban charity gave it overtones of philanthropic education for social deviants. Did the poor whose lives seemed most disrupted by industry and the city need systematic exposure to the lessons of the manual classroom or should it be required of all youth? The answer was ambiguous: everyone needed it, but especially the poor.

Despite the confusion inherent in the movement and the opposition of educators, manual training was clearly advancing. The eclectic forces which made the manual movement so influential at the end of the nineteenth century were united by several widely held beliefs—that industrialism had separated work and life, that moral values were in decline, and that the school should be the primary agent for reasserting the values of hard work and respect for labor. Of particular relevance to America's

[7] W. E. B. DuBois and August G. Dill (eds.), *The Negro American Artisan* (Atlanta, 1912), p. 121.

blacks and to the urban poor, manual education was expected to introduce practicality into schools, preserve traditional values, and enhance industrial progress. The persuasiveness of these arguments was evident: special manual education schools were established in a number of cities before 1890, and the same year a Bureau of Education survey of thirty-six cities reported thousands of students from elementary to high school grade engaged in drawing, cardboard construction, wood and metal work, sewing, and cooking. By the early twentieth century, few students would pass through the American educational system without some exposure to manual work.

FROM MANUAL TRAINING TO VOCATIONAL EDUCATION

The seeming prosperity of the manual training movement was ambiguous, however. By the turn of the century, the conditions which had been conducive to the development of manual training in the 1870's intensified. Industrialization had progressed still further in replacing skilled labor with machines tended by unskilled workers. Industrial growth brought immigrants to the city—from America's farms and from across the Atlantic—accentuating the problems of urban chaos and poverty. As the century began, urbanization had progressed to a point where 32.9% of the population lived in cities of more than 8,000, compared to 22.6% in 1880. Incorporations and mergers during the 1890's established the modern corporate structure of business; by 1900 there was little doubt that big business was the most powerful force in the country. Labor unions had grown as well, and had become more willing to engage in open battle for their rights. The violence surrounding the labor disputes of the 1880's and 90's heightened the feeling that society was in disarray. Finally, a generation of muckrakers brought these developments to the attention of a public increasingly concerned about the apparent disintegration of society.

Even as manual training was being introduced into the schools, it was becoming divorced from its original assumptions and falling victim to rapidly changing attitudes. The expectation that hand learning would profoundly alter pedagogical practices had proven false. Students continued to be taught in the same stultifying ways, except that tools now shared the curriculum with books. Educational psychology was also being revised. The transfer-of-training model upon which manual education had been predicated—the notion that the mind could be disciplined by knowledge of general principles applicable in any situation—was giving way to the idea that learning had to be specific and directed to immediate ends. In addition, growing doubt had appeared that manual education's social goals were attainable. The expectation that schools would alleviate the social problems of industrialism had proved unrealistic, and manual training as a social panacea thus came into disrepute.

The most basic problem confronting manual education, however, was its failure of economic relevance. Forced to deny its vocational applicability to gain widespread support, manual educators had consistently presented their innovation as a supplementary approach to traditional goals. At the same time, those seeking more drastic changes in the relationship between schools and the economy had begun to raise serious questions about manual training's economic and vocational utility. The emphasis on drawing, wood, and elementary metal work, they claimed, was misplaced in the new industrial order. The economy did not need individuals who understood the traditional crafts and the principles of production, but men to run the industrial machine, supervise the assembly line, and organize the corporation. Manual training had failed to show its practicality, and on this issue those committed to education for industrial efficiency broke with the earlier advocates of hand learning. (Doc. #4)

Finally, manual training lost support as the ideology of American reform and attitudes toward industrialism changed. After the turn of the century, the emphasis on the disruptions caused by industrial growth gave way to an acceptance and then an exaltation of industrialization. Reformers became less concerned with retaining traditional ways of life and more committed to channeling, rationalizing, and making more efficient the industrial process. The new attitudes affected every American institution—politics, business, social welfare, churches. This acceptance of industrialism led to new assumptions about schooling: industry "as a controlling factor in social progress" should have a significant influence on education, and in an industrial society marked by bureaucracy and hierarchy, formal schooling was necessary for upward mobility. Both assumptions strengthened calls for the greater integration of education and the economy. For manual training, the issue of relevance which had given the movement its initial impetus became its worst enemy, as the schools turned toward more specifically vocational training.

The manual training movement proved to be ephemeral, overtaken by vocational education only two decades after its inception. It was nevertheless important for its role in smoothing the transition to vocationalism in public education. Many of the arguments for manual training—its moral value, its efficacy in improving the lot of the poor and in integrating schooling with life—were consistent with previous ideology, and they were later taken up by advocates of vocational education. The purposes of manual training were ostensibly those of the common school, while its methods were those of vocational education. Hence, when national debate shifted from manual training to vocational education in the decade prior to 1900, the difference was not so much one of methods, content, or justification as one of purpose: where manual training had proposed to train the hand in order to perfect a general cultural education, vocational education intended to prepare its students for specific jobs. More than anything else, manual training changed the conception of what might legitimately be taught in the schools; once this was accomplished, the shift to vocational purposes seemed a logical development. The transition was eased by the contradictions inherent in the manual movement itself. But external forces—the pressure of businessmen for increased vocationalism, the continued industrialization and urbanization of the country, and the intensification of social problems which manual education appeared unable to solve—caused manual training as a compromise reform to be superseded.

ARGUMENTS FOR VOCATIONAL EDUCATION

Between 1890 and 1910, vocational education attracted the support of almost every group in the country with an interest in education. The magnitude of this conversion was overwhelming; it indicates that, in a period when large segments of society were conscious of the problems caused by industrialism, vocational education was almost universally perceived as a panacea. While manual training had attracted the passing attention of diverse segments of society, vocationalism held together a coalition

that included every group with any political power, and
even generated an association—the National Society for
the Promotion of Industrial Education (N.S.P.I.E.),
founded in 1906—to coordinate support. By 1917, the
movement had gained its greatest triumph—passage of
the Smith–Hughes Act granting federal funds for vocational training.

The drive for vocational education drew some of its
strongest and earliest support from the business community. Through the National Association of Manufacturers (N.A.M.), founded in 1895, through private trade
schools established as models for preparing trained
workers, and through their prominent role in the
N.S.P.I.E. and the drive for federal funding, businessmen provided both economic arguments and political
influence for vocationalism in education.

One of their initial arguments was the necessity for
highly skilled labor. The factory system had made the
apprenticeship system obsolete, businessmen alleged. It
was now difficult and economically inefficient to allow
informal, on-the-job learning in modern factories; hence
the scarcity of skilled workers could be alleviated only
through skill education. In reference to less skilled
labor, businessmen argued that better-trained workers
would be happier at their jobs because of increased
understanding and appreciation of their role in the
industrial economy, that industrial accidents, absentee-
ism, and labor turn-over would decrease, and that increased efficiency and output would be the result of a
happier, more stable work force. In particular, the
N.A.M. focused on the rise of Germany as a world power
and an international competitor, and pointed to the
German system of trade and continuation (part-time)
schools as the cause of that country's growth. The clear
implication was that the United States would have to

invest in vocational training to compete successfully in world markets. In this context, spokesmen for the economic benefits of industrial education described it as necessary in the natural historical development of the United States: previously the country had relied for its expansion on an abundance of natural resources; but with those dwindling it was necessary (and natural) to develop our *human* resources more fully through training a skilled work force. (Doc. #7)

An equally serious problem, according to the N.A.M., was that existing apprenticeship programs and job entry were under the control of unions. Businessmen argued that union restriction was harmful to *workers,* that it denied them freedom to find a job and was thus thoroughly undemocratic. Industrial education would, by providing an alternative method of training, weaken this aspect of union control; within the N.A.M., businessmen even argued that industrial education would weaken unionism as a whole. A closer look suggests, however, that union control over apprenticeships was largely ineffective; the rhetoric of its stand indicates that N.A.M. support for industrial education in the worker's interests was primarily a guise for its belligerently anti-union attitudes. (Doc. #7)

Although the anti-union bias of the N.A.M. irritated some other advocates of vocational education, the businessmen's argument that industrial values should dominate American education and that the schools should serve the requirements of the industrial economy soon became the prevailing ethic of the vocational education movement. Such arguments were incorporated into the influential *Report of the Commission on National Aid to Vocational Education* of 1914 almost precisely as businessmen had formulated them ten to fifteen years earlier. (Doc. #10)

The extent to which businessmen combined calls for vocationalism with hostility to unions influenced organized labor's attitude towards vocational training. Unions were already sensitive to anti-labor bias in public schools —in 1902 the A.F. of L. called for an investigation of teacher attitudes towards the children of workers—and they were highly critical of private trade schools which had been openly hostile to organized labor and had, in a few cases, provided students as strikebreakers. Hence organized labor tended to distrust vocational schools as "scab hatcheries," though without playing an active role in the early vocational education movement.

In 1908 the growing movement and the N.S.P.I.E. forced the A.F. of L. into a more positive stance. The reports of the Federation's Committee on Industrial Education, particularly in 1910, affirmed support for the principle of industrial education in the public schools, but revealed a great deal of ambivalence. Like the businessmen whom they distrusted, labor leaders felt that the old apprenticeship system had failed, and that America's future welfare depended on the industrial training of workers. Of course, unions saw trade training as benefiting workers rather than businessmen, through higher pay for greater skills. Like the educators whom they perceived to be under the influence of businessmen, union men decried the high dropout rate as detrimental to the welfare of workers. The position of labor in the vocational education movement was therefore an uneasy one. The A.F. of L. supported both full-time and part-time industrial education for those past the age of fourteen, but its emphasis was always on assuring that labor would have enough control to counteract the threat of business domination. It sought public rather than private sponsorship of vocational training, the participation of labor in all decision-making, and above all, the avoidance of extreme specialization. It thus hoped to avoid training for obsolescent jobs and prevent the business community's desires for skilled and efficient labor from being met at the expense of worker benefits. The position was best summarized by an A.F. of L. member in 1912: "We cannot stop the trend in the direction of this kind of education in the school; but we can, if we cooperate with the educators, have it come our way." [8] (Doc. #8)

At the deepest level, the ambivalence of labor toward vocational education reflected a long-standing conflict within the labor movement. On one side were those who sought improvements in the workers' standard of living, and who saw vocational education as a practical means towards this end. On the other were those who feared that vocational education would create a stratified school system, hampering mobility out of the working class. The final form of organized labor's support for vocational education appears due to the influence of Gompers and the ideals of business unionism which were moving organized labor toward accommodation with large scale industry. It also reflects, however, labor's assumption that it was not powerful enough to defeat a coalition of businessmen and educators, and would therefore have to concentrate on preventing business domination.

While business and labor focused on the economic returns from vocational training and on issues of control, educators defined their position in terms of a different set of problems. Foremost among these was the emergence of the high school as a mass institution. In 1890 less than 4% of the high school age population was enrolled in secondary schools; the percentage of

[8] Quoted in Berenice M. Fisher, *Industrial Education: American Ideals and Institutions* (Madison, 1967), pp. 127–128.

fourteen- to seventeen-year-olds in school had reached 28% by 1920 and 47% by 1930. Because those who had attended high school prior to 1890 tended to be middle class, secondary education had functioned to prepare students for social and economic leadership. After 1890, however, educators noted that those crowding into high school were different from previous students: they were the "children of the plain people," the "masses" as opposed to the "classes." The influx of working class and immigrant children threatened to destroy the high school's traditional function. Out of this condition came the question which would propel vocational education to the fore: what kind of secondary school education should these newcomers have? [9] Simultaneously, the nineteenth century rags-to-riches ideal, the notion that hard work and moral rectitude were sufficient for upward mobility, was being replaced by the belief that without formal schooling, individuals—particularly those from the working classes—would suffer in the race for success. The entry into the high school of the "children of the plain people" and the assumption of the increased importance of formal schooling raised the possibility that the newcomers might need an education peculiarly suited to their backgrounds and aspirations, but two additional phenomena—the dropout problem and the impact of business values on schoolmen— strengthened the perceived necessity for vocational education.

Tied to complaints over the slow progress children made through school and the problem of overaged youth, high attrition rates plagued educators committed to evolving a complete system of public schooling.

[9] See Edward A. Krug, *The Shaping of the American High School, 1880–1920* (New York, 1964), esp. Ch. 8.

Under the assumption that formal education was necessary for upward mobility, educators believed that those who left school at or before the minimum permissible age suffered in the labor market. Possessing neither education nor vocational skills, they suffered from the "wasted years" syndrome—the period between fourteen and sixteen when they could not engage in useful labor —and were victimized by "dead-end" jobs which offered no chance for advancement. Deplored as a waste of human resources, early school leaving was blamed not on economic necessity, but on conventional education's irrelevance to the future economic needs of most youth. (Doc. #5) Manual training, which had offered a similar critique of traditional education, had proved insufficient: it had become "a cultural subject mainly useful as a stimulus to other forms of intellectual effort—a sort of mustard relish, an appetizer—to be conducted without reference to any industrial end. It has been severed from real life as completely as have the other school activities." (Doc. #4) Finally, vocational educators argued that continuation in school under the traditional curriculum, a possibility under expanded compulsory attendance laws, would not provide most youth with any real mobility. The solution to the dropout problem required a curriculum specifically directed at future employment, one which would keep children in school because of its relevance to their futures.

Reinforcing this argument for vocationalism was the impact of business values and industrial ethics on schoolmen. Taking as their model the corporation's hierarchical and bureaucratic organization, educators introduced a wide range of administrative procedures and specialized departments into their school systems. Ideals of utilitarianism, efficient use of resources, and economy in production became by-words of educational management. The impact of these trends in terms of vocational education was two-fold. First, they intensified the commitment to integrating the school and the economy. Second, they justified a utilitarian diversification of the curriculum, one which would provide subject matter more closely related to the expected vocational careers of pupils. (Doc. #6)

While education which differentiated among students by prospective vocations would solve the most serious problems facing educators at the turn of the century, it contradicted a central tenet of the public schools: a common education for all students at each level of the system. While the nineteenth-century ideal of the common school was rarely attained—blacks and Indians were explicitly excluded, poverty generally prevented the full participation of working-class children, and differentiation had occurred in secondary schools—the goal of a system open to all remained, and by 1900 seemed closer to realization than ever before. Hence some of the most fundamental conflicts of vocational education were fought over the issue of commonality and democracy in education. What emerged was a redefinition of the idea of equality of educational opportunity and a rejection of the common school ideal.

The same forces which had led to advocacy of vocationalism thus served to justify the transition to a new concept of democracy in education. The dropout problem revealed that most children, especially among the poor, never completed high school. This implied that the common school system, rather than providing equal opportunity to all children, was discriminatory by its very nature:

Instead of affording equality of educational opportunity to all, the elementary school by offering but one course of instruction, and this of a literary character, serves the interests of but one type of children and in a measure the taste, capacity, and educational destination of all others, and of those, too, whose needs are imperative and to whom the future holds no further advantages. In a word, what was intended to be a school for the masses and afford equality of educational opportunity to all . . . serves well the interests of but the few.[10]

Additionally, the criterion of usefulness in education, of relevance to future occupations, implied that the common school system deprived many children of what they needed most from education. Under the redefinition of democracy in education implicit in these criticisms, every pupil had the right to, and the state was obligated to provide, education commensurate with his abilities and occupational future. Essential differences among children—socio-economic background, needs, abilities, aspirations—had to be recognized and instruction adapted to these differences; hence the differentiation of the curriculum into multiple occupational categories and the placing of students into the proper category became necessary. In essence, curricula differentiation, categorization of students by future economic roles, and the adjustment of the curriculum to the economic demands of the marketplace became the defining characteristics of public education. Only in this way could individuals on the fringes of society—the poor, racial minorities, the "manually-motivated"—be integrated into the educational system and then into the labor force; vocational education was first justified, then glorified, as the only basis upon which a mass educational system could be made democratic. (Docs. #13, 14)

The redefinition of equality of educational opportunity cleared the way for the triumph of vocationalism

[10] William H. Elson and Frank P. Bachman, "Different Courses for Elementary Schools," *Educational Review*, XXXIX (1910), 361.

in American education. Differentiation and categorization by future occupational role were now essential for a democratic educational system. When added to the arguments that vocational training would increase economic efficiency and growth, expand the possibilities of upward social mobility, assure the retention of pupils in school for longer periods of time, and teach more efficiently the moral values previously attributable to manual education, vocationalism had become a potent political force.

While economic arguments and a redefinition of equality of educational opportunity gave vocationalism its essential thrust, schoolmen continued to stress their responsibilities for moral training. Here the claims made for vocational education were similar to those made two decades earlier for manual training: in a society characterized by social unrest, moral decay, and increasing alienation from work, industrial education would reverse these tendencies by eradicating urban poverty and restoring pride and dignity to manual workers. Again, the most concrete result claimed for vocational education was success in reforming criminals, a claim previously made for manual training. Because crime was symptomatic of deeper problems caused by industrialization and urbanization, this argument carried great force; rather than stigmatizing a kind of education deemed appropriate to rehabilitating criminals, educators embraced vocational education as the best way of rehabilitating society as a whole.

Yet with the increased emphasis on vocational goals came a shift in the nature of the moral values to be inculcated. Writers still stressed the love of work and the sense of dignity which industrial education would instill, but now values specifically related to industrial work were accentuated: punctuality, discipline, submission to those in authority, recognition of the rights of others, and acceptance of one's place in the industrial process. In an era when reformers were becoming critical of the inhumanity of industrial work, the response of public education was to adapt the individual to the new industrial system so as to make him happy with his work and proud of his position in society. Educators accepted the nature of technology as given, and strove to accommodate their pupils to industrialism in the most direct way possible.

The moral arguments for vocational training were particularly convincing to social reformers. Urban social workers supported vocational education because its promises were congruent with their goals of alleviating urban poverty and coping with morally degrading conditions in urban slums. For the advocates of child welfare and compulsory education, the moral elements of knowing a trade were intertwined with the goal of keeping children in schools longer. Extended schooling, vocational training, and moral rectitude all seemed peculiarly interrelated.

With the support of agrarian groups, who were also seeking education more relevant to their economic needs, the vocational education movement had become a powerful political coalition. Nowhere was this more evident than in the drive for federal funding. Coordinated by the National Society for the Promotion of Industrial Education, the battle for federal aid revealed the diversity and the strength of the vocational movement. Although vocationalism was growing—a 1910 survey showed programs in twenty-nine states—the Society argued that only federal aid could accelerate the trend, standardize programs, and ultimately legitimize vocationalism as integral to public education. Toward this end the Society, and especially its secretary, Charles A. Prosser, directed its attention.

The year 1910 marked something of a turning point; by then the N.E.A., the N.A.M., and the A.F. of L. had all issued major reports supporting vocational education in the public schools. Between 1910 and 1914 political support accelerated, and in the latter year Congress appointed the Commission on National Aid to Vocational Education to explore the topic and come up with recommendations. The conclusions of the report had almost been predetermined. The Commission's four congressional members had all previously declared themselves in favor of federal aid; the five other members were active in the N.S.P.I.E. and included Charles Prosser. Indeed, the Commission's major problems lay in how to justify the aid it proposed and to elaborate the expenditure and administration of the funds. Although it undertook extensive hearings at which opposition to federal funding appeared—usually from educators fearful of federal involvement—much of the Commission's information was provided by the Society and Prosser. Not surprisingly, then, the Commission found a "great and crying need" for vocational education and recommended that federal funds be made available to meet this need. The justifications were all familiar: the need to enhance national productivity in the face of international competition, the increment to the individual's earning power, the stability of a trained work force, and the establishment of true equality of educational opportunity that vocationalism would bring. One relatively new theme appeared, necessary to rationalize federal involvement in education: in a highly mobile society, localities could not afford to train youth for work who would seek employment elsewhere. Training for a national labor market required federal support.[11] (Doc. #10)

Committed to federal funding even before it met, the Commission's recommendations were general enough to retain the political coalition now moving toward federal financing. Grants were to be given to the states for the training of teachers in agricultural, trade and industrial, and home economics subjects, and for paying supervisor and teacher salaries in these areas. Only public schools of "less than college grade" and for those over fourteen would receive aid. Three kinds of schools were eligible: all-day schools devoting half time to "actual practice for a vocation"; part-time schools for young workers over fourteen to extend their vocational knowledge, prepare them for entry into a vocation, or "extend the general civic or vocational intelligence of the pupils"; and vocational evening schools for adult workers. The Commission also proposed a Federal Board for Vocational Education responsible for channeling funds to state boards and the requirement that grants be made on a matching basis.

With the Commission's report, the movement quickly came to a culmination. Passage of the Smith–Lever Act in 1914 provided federal funds for agricultural extension programs and assured agrarian support for vocational education. The outbreak of war in Europe increased the pressure; vocational training became part of President Wilson's preparedness campaign. In February of 1917, just two months before America's entry into World

[11] While the Commission attempted to establish a history of federal involvement in education where national economic needs were at stake and where localities could not provide the resources —the implications of which were never fully spelled out—it was clear that the report broke new ground in federal-state educational relations.

War I, the Smith–Hughes Act providing federal aid to vocational education was passed, legislating the recommendations of the 1914 Commission with only slight modifications. (Doc. #11)

Smith–Hughes culminated more than a decade's agitation and formalized the structure of vocational education. The coalition that had sponsored it drew together almost every major interest group in the country, including several (such as business and labor) that generally saw themselves as enemies, not partners. The early struggle for control among these various groups was resolved by naming the Secretaries of Commerce, Labor, and Agriculture and the Commissioner of Education to the Federal Board for Vocational Education, along with three citizens representing agriculture, labor, and commerce and industry. Primary responsibility for overseeing the expansion of vocational education was in the hands of the Board, although the Bureau of Education, the N.E.A., labor unions, and the N.S.P.I.E. (renamed in 1920 the National Society for Vocational Education) also played active roles in developing curricula and teaching methods, training instructors, and otherwise working out the system's details.

Several factors combined to severely limit the discretion of the Board. The Smith–Hughes Act determined maximum amounts which could be disbursed to each state, and specified additional restrictions on what could be used for agricultural, home economics, and trade and industrial courses, teacher training, and part-time education. The federal legislation also mandated a narrow conception of vocational education, one which tended to further "the idea that instruction, to be effective, must be very specific and narrowly related to the occupational skills it seeks to develop," and which discouraged experimentation with a broader concept of vocational education. Hence the program mandated by Smith–Hughes sharply distinguished between vocational and academic education, thereby strengthening and legitimizing the evolving dual system of education. (Doc. #17) As a result of the various limitations, the main work of the Board consisted of advising states and communities wishing to establish vocational education programs, administering the routine disbursement of funds, and publishing the results of research and experimental programs developed by the Board and others.

Federal aid was never intended to cover the costs of vocational education, but rather to serve as "seed money" to motivate the states into developing their own programs. This was the logic behind the requirement that the states match federal aid dollar for dollar. In fact, most states spent more than the minimum required; in 1917–18, when the federal allotment totaled $1,655,587, federal aid represented 27% of expenditure on vocational education, 20% of expenditure on industrial and trade education, and .1% of total expenditures for public education; by 1925–26, when the allotment leveled off at $7,184,902, federal aid represented 24%, 23%, and .3% respectively. While the Board's activities may have been important from the viewpoint of providing guidance and research, federal aid was not itself critical to the existence of vocational education.

Federal aid, moreover, did not appear to stimulate increased participation in full-time vocational courses. In 1912–13, after industrial education had been generally accepted but before federal funding was in effect, 6.9% of high school students were enrolled in industrial and trade courses; in 1924, when utilization of federal aid was near its peak, 6.7% of high school students were in such courses. By 1930, 13% of rural boys age fifteen to eighteen were in some form of agricultural education, 4.6% of urban boys were in trade and industrial courses, and 4.1% of girls were in home economics courses.

But these statistics reflect only the continued low enrollments in all-day schools. Federal aid had considerably stronger impact on part-time education. In 1912–13, Wisconsin was the only state with any part-time schools. Six years later, seventeen states had laws making some form of part-time education compulsory for those dropping out of school at fourteen. An additional seventeen states passed such laws by 1928. In 1919, 86% of pupils in federally-aided trade or industrial schools were in part-time programs; by 1924 this had increased to 92%. One impact of Smith–Hughes was thus to make vocational training predominantly part-time.

The relatively low enrollments in full-time vocational training programs are misleading, however, in assessing the full impact of the vocational movement on American education. The triumph of vocationalism lay less in the numbers enrolled in trade training courses than in the belief that the primary goal of schooling was to prepare youth for the job market, in the redefinition of equality of educational opportunity that accompanied the differentiated curriculum, and in growth of vocational guidance, educational testing, and the junior high school to select students more effectively for educational programs on the basis of their predicted future economic roles. (Doc. #12) Vocationalism's importance thus extended far beyond the confines of the vocational classroom, for its assumptions and practices pervaded the education system. This can be seen in the conflicts that emerged following passage of the Smith–Hughes Act.

VOCATIONALISM AND CONFLICT

National organizations—the N.A.M., the N.E.A., the N.S.P.I.E., the A.F. of L., and organized agrarian groups like the Grange—shaped the arguments and influenced the drive for federal financing. Once these groups had agreed to the principle of vocationalism in the schools and had redefined educational opportunity so as to accommodate vocationalism in public education, the major battles had been to convince those fearful of federal involvement of the necessity for federal aid. The dominance of national organizations meant that unorganized individuals had little say about the acceptance or structure of vocational education—only a minority of workers were represented by the A.F. of L., and the urban poor had a voice only indirectly, through non-enrollment in vocational courses. Because the vocational movement had come to be dominated by national groups, it appears to have been marked by little conflict after 1910.

However, this ignores the conflicts that vocational education generated at the state and local level, where the dominance of national organizations was diluted and where conflicts of interest were more clearly delineated in the process of implementing the principle of vocational education. Conflict at the state and local level usually revolved around two basic issues. The first was the question of who would control vocational training, under what conditions, and toward what ends. The second involved whether vocational education offered equality of educational opportunity, as its advocates claimed, or whether it was simply a mechanism of social class stratification offering second-class education.

The question of control had always existed. Initially, businessmen had argued for private schools run in their own interests, and in fact a number of the country's largest corporations sponsored their own training schools. As vocationalism gained strength, however, conflict focused on the control of publically-sponsored vocational programs. Following the recommendations of the Douglas Commission in 1906, Massachusetts appointed a Commission on Industrial Education to administer independent public vocational schools, a policy followed by Wisconsin in 1911. On a small scale, many districts instituted vocational high schools that were separate from the academic high schools. Claiming the need to keep vocational training from being undermined by academic educators, the prohibitive cost of industrial equipment, and the requirement of close contact between vocational programs and local industry, the proponents of separate schools stressed narrow vocational training, the teaching of skills specific to particular jobs. Their assumption was straight-forward: only separate, independent, public schools would keep vocational education truly vocational.

Opposition to separate schools was formidable and ultimately victorious. Educators, threatened by loss of control over a significant portion of the educational system, attacked separation for its excessive vocationalism and argued that it would produce workers at the expense of larger citizenship training. Organized labor feared that independent schools would be dominated by local business and used to flood the labor market without any consideration of the workers' long-term interests. Worst of all, however, separate vocational training violated a fundamental concept of democracy in public education, explicitly dividing rather than integrating America's diverse population. Fearful that students would be locked into vocational categories with little opportunity to compare curricula or to change their minds about further education or future occupational roles, critics argued that separation would hit hardest those vocational education had been aimed at—the working class and the poor—for it would further undermine their opportunities for mobility. Hence the questions of control ultimately became questions of opportunity and democracy, with both issues central to the battle over separate versus comprehensive high schools.

Nowhere was this more evident than in Chicago, where conflict over a "dual system" of education attracted nationwide attention. Under the sponsorship of the Chicago Association of Commerce, the city's former superintendent of schools Edwin G. Cooley drafted a bill in 1912 to divide Illinois' educational system into vocational and general schooling after grade six. Cooley reiterated the prevailing ideas about industrialism's impact on work, and he made clear that Americans would have to accept a society in which mobility had now become limited. But Cooley also claimed that in an industrial economy jobs themselves were neither meaningless nor alienating. Rather such ideas were products of attitudes inculcated by the existing educational system and by worker frustration over lack of technological skills. Teaching individuals how to increase their productivity, he declared, would increase their happiness: "Joy in work—is an absolute essential to contentment, happiness, honesty, and self-respect." [12] Using examples drawn from Germany, Cooley called for separate boards of vocational education and for special local taxation for vocational

[12] Edwin G. Cooley, "Professor Dewey's Criticism of the Chicago Commercial Club and Its Vocational Education Bill," *Vocational Education*, III (1913–14), 25.

training. "Separate schools" Cooley told the Chicago
Commercial Club

are necessary whose equipment, corps of teachers, and board
of administration must be in the closest possible relation to
the occupations. In such schools the applications of general
education to vocational work can be made only by men who
know the vocations . . . Such schools should be separate,
independent, compulsory day schools, supported by special
taxes, carried on usually in special buildings, administered by
special boards of practical men and women, taught by specially trained practical men from the vocations, and securing
the closest possible cooperation between the school and the
factory, the school and the farm, the school and the counting-
room, or the school and the home. (Doc. #15)

Brought before the state legislature in 1913 and in
subsequent years with the support of almost every major
business organization in Illinois, the proposed legislation
aroused a storm of protest before finally being defeated.
Chicago's superintendent of schools Ella Flagg Young,
one of the country's most respected and innovative educators, was worried about schools to train factory workers:
"If the schoolroom with its work bench and its dressmaking and millinery shops isn't something over and
beyond the mere factory workroom . . . we shall have
a system of education entirely wrong." [13] John Dewey
argued that the Cooley bill would wastefully divide and
duplicate educational administration, would continue a
philosophy that distinguished between training for the
leisured class and for the working class, and would leave
academic schooling remote "from the urgent realities of
contemporary life" while severely narrowing the scope
of vocational training. Dewey's essential criticisms, however, were that a dual system struck at the heart of

[13] Ella Flagg Young, "Educational Notes," *Catholic Educational
Review*, V (1913), 161–162.

democracy itself and abdicated any responsibility for reforming the industrial system. Terming it "the greatest evil now threatening the interests of democracy in education," he contended that separate vocational schools would isolate, stigmatize, and fix in predetermined places the children of America's working class. "The kind of vocational education in which I am interested is not one which will 'adapt' workers to the existing industrial regime; I am not sufficiently in love with the regime for that. It seems to me that the business of all who would not be educational time servers is . . . to strive for a kind of vocational education which will first alter the existing industrial system, and ultimately transform it." [14] (Doc. #16)

While Dewey joined the fray through the printed word, the political struggle was carried on by Chicago's Federation of Labor, an organization of the city's labor unions considerably more radical than the American Federation of Labor. Labor castigated the Cooley bill as an effort by large employers "to turn the public schools into an agency for providing them with an adequate supply of docile, well-trained and capable workers" and claimed that it would create "a caste system of education which would shunt the children of the laboring classes at an early age first into vocational courses and then into the factories." Marshalling widespread public support, including prominent social reformers and most of the city's teachers, the Federation's extensive lobbying campaigns proved successful. Despite its powerful backers, the Cooley bill failed to pass, and by 1920 was a dead issue.[15]

---

[14] John Dewey, "Splitting Up the School System," *The New Republic*, II (1915), 283–284; *ibid.*, III (1915), 42.

[15] George S. Counts, *School and Society in Chicago* (New York, 1928), Chs. viii–ix.

Yet if an explicitly segregated school system along future occupational lines was rejected in favor of comprehensive secondary schools, the idea that schools should differentiate and select out students for the marketplace remained strong. Moreover, the equation of vocational opportunity with social class background—the fundamental issue to the Chicago Federation of Labor—remained an issue. Within a few years after the demise of the Cooley bill, Chicago was divided over the introduction of the junior high school and educational testing, and again organized labor fought the reforms on the basis of early and inequitable selection of working class children for a working class education. "Here we have exactly the division proposed in the Cooley Bill," the Illinois State Federation of Labor declared in 1924, ". . . the purpose of which was to classify the children at the age of twelve years into two separate groups, one of which was destined for higher education and the other for industrial life." [16] Two years earlier, George S. Counts had affirmed that the Federation's fears were well-founded. In the *Selective Character of American Secondary Education,* Counts found that children advanced to high school and chose curricula largely on the basis of their father's occupation.

As a rule, those groups which are poorly represented in the high school patronize the more narrow and practical curricula, the curricula which stand as terminal points in the educational system and which prepare for wage-earning. And the poorer their representation in high school, the greater is the probability that they will enter these curricula. The one- and two-year vocational courses, wherever offered, draw their registration particularly, from the ranks of labor.[17]

[16] *Ibid.,* p. 174.
[17] George S. Counts, *The Selective Character of American Secondary Education* (Chicago, 1922), p. 143.

Counts' hope that secondary education would become universal was soon realized. But his pleas for differentiation on some basis other than social class were not. Americans found in the comprehensive high school an institution which met the demands of democracy, ostensibly providing all with the opportunity to succeed, while nonetheless differentiating by future vocational role and social class background.[18]

In sum, vocational education served two concrete purposes—to fasten the ideal of education for vocational goals onto the educational system, and to restructure the high school. It served to break down the common school ideology and the practice of a common educational system for all pupils; after vocational education had differentiated pupils according to future occupations, other forms of differentiation—ability-grouping being the most widespread—were introduced into the schools. Testing and vocational guidance were developed in order to administer the increasingly differentiated system. The high school of 1890 was fundamentally different from that of 1920. It had become a mass institution, and in the process had generated a change in the nature of education which enabled it to cope with the influx of students—to integrate them into the educational system and theoretically into the labor force—and to maintain a rough differentiation by social class.

Furthermore, there are strong indications that these two functions were the primary results of the vocational education movement. The economic promises of vocationalism failed to materialize. Listless students, particularly in trade and industrial programs, raised considerable

[18] See, *e.g.*, August B. Hollingshead, *Elmtown's Youth: The Impact of Social Classes on Adolescents* (New York, 1949), pp. 168–172, 192–203.

doubts about the economic benefits of most vocational training. Even during the movement's most expansive phase, some educators and industrialists doubted that formal schooling alone could provide the training necessary in an industrial economy. Many employers called for part-time industrial education combined with on-the-job training, a combination which appeared to be more effective than full-time vocational education—as evidenced by the increased enrollments in part-time programs after 1917 and by the resort to manpower programs in the 1960's. After 1917 complaints about the efficacy of vocational education continue to be heard, and alternatives to public training—corporation schools and private trade schools run by employers' associations and unions—remained available.

A NOTE ON THE VOCATIONAL EDUCATION OF FEMALES

The education of females has always had an uneasy place in vocational education. Women had been entering the job market in increasing numbers, thereby raising issues prominently discussed in the vocational movement as a whole: efficient use of resources, economic mobility, the adjustment of the school curriculum to job expectations. More important, however, was the concern that job entry was undermining the traditional roles of females as wives and mothers and that vocational training for the labor market might further this destructive process. In addition, women tended to remain in the marketplace for briefer periods than men, and any extensive vocational training was seen as economically wasteful. Out of this emerged a two-fold compromise. First, where vocational training was given, it focused on occupations defined as female. At the turn of the century, this meant training in dressmaking, millinery, and cooking; after 1920, the predominant training was in secretarial skills. Second, vocational courses were made to center as much as possible on home economics or domestic science. Any skill—sewing and cooking have been the most widespread—that *could* offer returns in the job market was doubly valuable if it led to better home management. While vocational training was thus made available to women, it was limited to certain areas, and was invariably subordinate to their larger role as homemakers. (Doc. #9)

VOCATIONAL EDUCATION, 1920–1970

Since the Smith–Hughes Act of 1917, the shape of vocational education has been heavily influenced by federal legislation. The George–Reed (1929), George–Ellzey (1934), and George–Dean (1936) Acts increased federal funding from an original seven million dollars available under Smith–Hughes to twenty-one million, while the latter also made distributive education eligible for federal support. In 1946, building upon the enthusiasm generated for vocational education during World War II, the George–Barden Act was passed, this time allocating thirty-six million dollars in federal aid and introducing some flexibility in the use of funds by the states. Not until the Vocational Education Act of 1963 and the subsequent amendments of 1968, however, were any substantive changes in federal support made. These greatly increased appropriations, introduced noncategorical grants allowing states flexibility in the development of programs, and attempted to tie vocational funding to manpower and job retraining programs.

Although some have seen in these developments a fundamental change in the concept of vocational education, the historical continuity in the issues raised is more striking. Conflict over what vocational education should emphasize—that is, over the relative importance of specific job training versus more general academic and skill education—continued. The purposes of vocational education have also remained closely tied to adapting the labor force to changes in the requirements of jobs and to helping certain groups become fully integrated into the economy.

The depression of the 1930's focused particular attention on vocational education as a solution to unemployment, with various New Deal programs—the Civilian Conservation Corps, the National Youth Administration, and the Works Project Administration—offering non-school vocational training. However, dissatisfaction and controversy surrounding passage of the George–Dean Act of 1936 led President Roosevelt to appoint a national committee to review the development of vocational education since 1917.

The committee's major findings were issued in 1938 in a report written by John D. Russell, Professor of Education at the University of Chicago. The Russell report noted with approval that federal aid had facilitated the extension and improvement of vocational training and had served to change the attitude of many educators towards vocationalism. But by promoting an overly-narrow concept of vocational education, preparing students for a limited range of occupations, encouraging dual educational systems, and complicating local school administration, Smith–Hughes and its successors were found to be seriously deficient. Inadequate guidance and placement services diluted the influence vocational training was having in the labor market. More specifically, the report claimed that while agricultural education and home economics had at least served the purposes for which they were instituted, trade and industrial education showed no sign of economic value. In an appendix to the report, two labor leaders charged with evaluating the effectiveness of industrial education found both employers and unions convinced of failure: industrial training failed to correspond to available jobs, while a "caste system" relating social class and school curriculum had developed. Several examples were given of employers who preferred to hire students from the general rather than industrial curriculum and then train them, on the grounds that such students learned better and were better behaved. Finally, the commission noted labor's complaint that it had not been consulted in the development of vocational education—evidence that conflict over power had not yet been resolved. (Doc. #17)

Despite this extensive list of criticisms, the Russell report reaffirmed the principle of vocational education in the public schools. It repeated arguments developed some thirty years earlier, concluded that vocational training would increase in the future, and recommended that it be made more general and more flexible. The report had little impact, however. Under the emergency conditions of World War II, specific skill training was linked to national defense, and by December 1941 more than one and a half million workers were receiving vocational training, many in schools running twenty-four hours a day. With the war's end, Congress passed the George–Barden Act of 1946 increasing federal aid to thirty-six million dollars annually.

During the late 1940's and early 1950's the vocational movement took on a more generalized form, especially as an aspect of Life Adjustment Education. Receiving its initial impetus in 1945 from Charles A. Prosser, a major figure in vocational education since the first decade of the twentieth century, the life adjustment movement articulated two continuing themes: (1) America's schools were failing to educate a majority of its youth, in this case the sixty per cent who were neither being prepared for college nor for skilled trades under existing vocational programs, and (2) the schools could only correct this condition by redirecting education toward more practical ends. Assuming that "life adjustment is impossible unless occupational adjustment occurs," the movement sought to make all schooling stand a test of immediate relevance to daily problem solving. Formalized by the appointment of two national commissions on life adjustment in 1947 and 1950, the movement initially received widespread support but was quickly subjected to harsh criticism. Offering little that was new, life adjustment education soon became for critics a caricature of anti-intellectualism in American life and of the status quo in American society.[19] (Doc. #18)

For much of the 1950's, then, vocational education either was on the defensive or received scant attention. In the early sixties, however, the subject once again became prominent in educational circles. High unemployment rates continued to prevail among untrained workers and there was recognition that the accelerating pace of technological change was making many jobs obsolete. (Doc. #19) A new national commission was appointed by President Kennedy in 1961, and its report, like the 1938 Russell report, sharply criticized existing vocational programs for their insensitivity to changes in the labor market and to the needs of large segments of the population. The commission's recommendations, legislated in the Vocational Education Act of 1963,

---

[19] U.S. Office of Education, *Life Adjustment Education for Every Youth*, Bulletin No. 22, 1951, p. 83. A major criticism of life adjustment can be found in Arthur Bestor, *Educational Wastelands* (Urbana, 1953).

attempted to redirect vocational training by broadening its scope and flexibility and by focusing on the economically and educationally disadvantaged. States were now allowed to transfer federal appropriations from one occupational category to another; urban states could thus apply their agricultural education funds to industrial training. Viewed as an initial phase of the "war on poverty," the act was also designed to reach those outside the labor market and those discriminated against because of their lack of skills, and funds were therefore made available for programs designed to fit individuals for gainful employment.[20]

The 1963 legislation also created an Advisory Commission on Vocational Education to evaluate the law's operation. The report of that commission, submitted in 1967, showed little evidence that the act's two major objectives had been achieved, because of its permissive nature and the lack of concerted effort to overcome resistance to change. By 1967, the problems of technological unemployment and of poverty among minority groups were perceived as even more serious. The result was the passage of the Vocational Education Amendments of 1968, reaffirming the federal commitment to a more general concept of vocational education and to the problems of the disadvantaged. (Doc. #20)

Thus, since 1917 there has been a shift in federal legislation away from the narrow skill training embodied in the Smith–Hughes Act and toward broader conceptions of vocationalism, including technical education and basic literacy skills. During the early 1970's, yet another approach to vocationalism was proposed— career education. Most prominently advocated by U.S.

[20] Panel of Consultants on Vocational Education, *Education for a Changing World of Work* (Washington, D.C., 1963).

Commissioner Sidney P. Marland, career education was offered as an innovative concept designed to make American education more relevant to the lives and needs of young people. Yet many of its elements had been evident in earlier reform movements, notably its emphasis on adapting all school experiences toward practical and occupational ends. As proposed by Commissioner Marland, career education would teach job skills as well as refocus "classes in the basic subject areas—math, science, language arts, and social studies—in such a way that these classes were presented in terms of the student's career interests." In the effort to meet the needs of those for whom the educational system was judged to be failing, career education called for the reorganization of schooling so that it would bear directly and specifically on the student's planned career. (Doc. #21)

Despite the innovations of the 1960's and early 1970's, the arguments and conflicts remained remarkably similar to those which raged at the beginning of the century. The following statement, published in 1971, echoed views articulated seventy years earlier:

If students are not motivated toward the acquisition of adequate education, we will face an increasing waste of our human resources, continued riots in the streets, and a general deterioration of society. Except for the relatively small number of students who even now seek learning for its own sake, students will be motivated to learn only if their schooling is relevant to their lives, to their ambitions, and to their styles of learning. Vocational education speaks to the need for relevancy. . . . Society has rarely been disappointed when it looked to the educational profession for the solution of some of its most pressing problems.[21]

[21] Marvin Feldman, "Comprehensive Education: Redefined for a Humanist Society," in Gerald Somers and J. Kenneth Little, *Vocational Education: Today and Tomorrow* (Madison, 1971), p. 346.

The "pressing problems" of the sixties were those of technological unemployment and the poverty of minority groups. Those of the turn of the century were perceived to be the need to integrate immigrants and the "children of the plain people" into the schools and the labor force, provide a substitute for a once viable apprenticeship system, and compete successfully in world markets. At both times the basic principle was the same: vocational education could serve as the solution to immediate economic problems and as the mechanism for integrating those threatening the tranquility of schools and society.

Similarly, there were several points common to the criticisms of vocational education—charges of its narrowness and inability to keep pace with the demands of the economy, its creation of dual educational systems, and its stifling of equality of educational opportunity for the working class and the poor. Beyond these charges, even the economic justification for vocational education was weakened by evaluations in the 1960's. Although the results were somewhat ambiguous, most studies found vocational education to have no long-term economic benefits, as measured by income, job stability, and employment rates. Several reported that vocational graduates had great difficulty obtaining work in the occupation for which they had been trained, usually because their training had little relevance to the local labor market.[22] Federal legislation thus continued to affirm

[22] An enormous body of material has appeared on the efficacy of vocational education, much of it highly technical and often statistically inadequate. The literature is surveyed in Jacob J. Kaufman, "The Role of Vocational Education in the Transition from School to Work," in Arnold Weber, Frank Cassell, and Woodrow Ginsberg (eds.), *Public-Private Manpower Policies* (Madison, 1969); J. Kenneth Little, *Review and Synthesis on the Place-*

the place of vocational education in public schooling, despite little evidence that such schooling actually provided equality of educational opportunity. There was in 1972, as in 1917, no strong economic argument for vocational education; justification for its existence must be found elsewhere.

CONCLUSION

The continuity of the debates and the uncertainty over the impact of vocational education should not obscure the momentous impact vocationalism has had on America's schools. While its actual place in the curriculum has always been less than its advocates desired, and while it has invariably been accorded second class citizenship and has never enrolled more than a small percentage of the total school age population, vocational education has been a major force in the reconstruction of the American school. The nineteenth-century expansion of educational opportunity had been predicated on notions of commonality, the inculcation of moral values, and the expectation that knowledge broadly applied would enhance industrial progress. At the turn of the century, however, an ideology emerged that demanded explicit ties between schooling and the occupational structure. The traditional emphasis on industriousness, thrift, and sobriety was supplemented by a commitment to instruction in job skills and to the categorization of youth by their future occupational roles. The trend was revealed by Helen and Robert Lynd in their study of Muncie, Indiana, during the mid-1920's: "specific tool and skill activities in factory, home, and office" had be-

ment and Follow-up of Vocational Education Students (Columbus, 1970); and Garth Mangum, Reorienting Vocational Education (Ann Arbor, 1968).

come the most prominent feature of the city's high school. The president of Muncie's Board of Education cogently summarized the importance of vocationalism when he declared: "For a long time all boys were trained to be President. Then for a while we trained them all to be professional men. Now we are training boys to get jobs." [23]

The transformation in goals was accompanied by radical changes in the methodology of public education. Once the principle of preparation for economic roles was accepted, curricula and students had to be differentiated. Schools were now required to provide a variety of "relevant" courses and students had to be chosen for their particular roles. The former intensified pressure on the schools to respond to almost any real or fancied social need. The latter raised the serious questions of who was to be chosen for which curriculum and how they were to be chosen. These issues gave powerful force to the evolving educational testing, guidance, and junior high school movements, all of which seemed to provide more opportunities for choice, greater objectivity in selection, and more individualized *and* more efficient methods of running the schools. Seeking to resolve the problem of how to absorb the "children of the plain people" flooding secondary education after 1890, vocationalism and its spinoffs established a new definition of equality of educational opportunity which focused on the "evident and probable destinies" of youth, and which furnished the justification for mechanisms tending to segregate pupils by class.

The impact of vocationalism also revealed the extent to which American education had accepted the ethics

[23] Helen and Robert Lynd, *Middletown* (New York, 1929), pp. 194–196.

of the emerging corporate order. Vocational education was part of a broader rationalization of the schools, which included specialization of function, cost accounting, research and testing departments, and development of a science of administration. The ideal school system had come to be modeled after the modern corporation, both in its hierarchical and bureaucratic organization and in its purpose; students were raw materials to be processed in an efficiently run plant, and the criterion of success was the price the finished product could bring in the market place. Hence the enthusiastic acceptance of vocational education into the public schools, despite its contradiction of earlier ideals, paralleled the enthusiastic acceptance by educators of the industrial order. With the vocational education movement, educators saw their role as serving the industrial order and adapting students to its requirements. Economic criteria had become a primary force in educational decision-making.

Bibliographical Note

The writing of the history of vocational education has been largely hortatory, designed to elicit support for vocationalism in the public schools. Recently, however, historians have begun to place the subject in the context of other educational developments. Lawrence A. Cremin, *The Transformation of the School* (New York, 1961); Henry J. Perkinson, *The Imperfect Panacea: American Faith in Education, 1865–1965* (New York, 1968); Edward A. Krug, *The Shaping of the American High School, 1880–1920* (New York, 1964) and *The Shaping of the American High School, 1920–1941* (Madison, 1972); and David K. Cohen and Marvin Lazerson, "Education and the Corporate Order," *Socialist Revolution,* II (March–April, 1972), 47–72 relate vocational education to larger changes in American education. Berenice M. Fisher, *Industrial Education: American Ideals and Institutions* (Madison, 1967) and Sol Cohen, "The Industrial Education Movement, 1906–1917," *American Quarterly,* XX (1968), 95–110 specifically focus on vocationalism itself, while W. Richard Stephens, *Social Reform and the Origins of Vocational Guidance* (Washington, D.C., 1970) treats one ramification of the vocational movement. Marvin Lazerson, *Origins of the Urban School: Public Education in Massachusetts, 1870–1915* (Cambridge, 1971) is a valuable case study of manual and vocational education in one state. Vocationalism was closely tied to the drive for efficiency in education, a movement described in Raymond A. Callahan, *Education and the Cult of Efficiency* (Chicago, 1962).

A number of older works written by advocates of vocational education remain useful in giving a sense of what the movement was about. The best of these are Charles A. Bennett, *History of Manual and Industrial Education up to 1870* (Peoria, 1926) and *History of Manual and Industrial Education, 1870–1917* (Peoria, 1937); Ray M. Stombaugh, *A Survey of the Movements Culminating in Industrial Art Education* (New York, 1936); and Layton S. Hawkins, Charles A. Prosser, and John C. Wright, *Development of Vocational Education* (Chicago, 1951).

The most influential writings on manual training are those of Calvin M. Woodward, especially *Manual Education* (St. Louis, 1878) and *The Manual Training School* (Boston, 1887), and of John D. Runkle, whose "The Manual Element in Education" was originally published in the *41st Annual Report of the Massachusetts Board of Education* (Boston, 1878). Isaac E. Clark, *Art and Industry* (Forty-Sixth Congress, U.S. Senate, Executive Documents, 1897) contains an enormous amount of material on the manual training movement.

The best way of studying the vocational movement after 1900 is through the publications of the various interest groups. The bulletins and pamphlets of the National Society for the Promotion of Industrial Education (renamed in 1920 the National Society for Vocational Education) are indispensable for understanding the arguments for expanded vocational education. The National Education Association *Journal of Proceedings and Addresses* reveals the concerns and conflicts which underlay the professional educator's approach to vocationalism. The best sources for business attitudes toward vocational education are the annual proceedings of the

National Association of Manufacturers and the National Association of Corporation Schools. Organized labor's position can be found in the annual proceedings of the American Federation of Labor.

Studies and reports published by federal and state governments are also valuable. The bibliographies of U.S. Office of Education publications on vocational education, found in that Office's *Bulletins,* No. 22 (1937) and No. 3 (1960), are good starting points for federal material. The 17th and 25th annual reports of the U.S. Commissioner of Labor, entitled *Trade and Technical Education* (1902) and *Industrial Education* (1910), are examples of other government documents. The most influential of the state commission reports was the Massachusetts Commission on Industrial and Technical Education, *Report* (Boston, 1906), frequently referred to as the Douglas Commission. Also of interest are the reports of the New Jersey Commission on Industrial Education (1909), the Michigan State Commission on Industrial and Agricultural Education (1910), and the Wisconsin Commission on the Plans for the Extension of Industrial and Agricultural Training (1911).

One of the primary arguments for vocational training in the schools was the inefficiency and waste resulting from early school leaving, a fact documented in Leonard Ayres' highly influential study *Laggards in Our Schools* (New York, 1909). Two excellent sources summarizing and describing the condition of vocational education in the first decade of the twentieth century are the American Academy of Political and Social Science, *Industrial Education* (Philadelphia, 1909) and Frank M. Leavitt, *Examples of Industrial Education* (Boston, 1912). Vocational educators frequently wrote in support of their cause; their position was ably summarized by Charles A. Prosser and Charles R. Allen, *Vocational Education in a*

Democracy (New York, 1925). A recent biography of one of the country's most influential vocational educators i Walter H. Drost, *David Snedden and Education for So cial Efficiency* (Madison, 1967).

Between 1910 and 1917 the major focus of the voca tional movement was on securing federal aid, a process carefully documented in Lloyd E. Blauch, *Federal Coop eration in Agricultural Extension Work, Vocational Edu cation, and Vocational Rehabilitation,* U.S. Office of Education, Bulletin No. 15 (1933). The major arguments for such aid were laid out in the report of the Commission on National Aid to Vocational Education (Sixty-Third Congress, U.S. House of Representatives, 1914) which led to the passage of the Smith–Hughes Act. Federal activities after Smith–Hughes are best documented in the bulletins and annual reports of the Federal Board of Vocational Education. In addition, the Office of Education published many studies concerning the implementation of vocational education in its Bulletins. The annual reports of the U.S. Commissioner of Education and the biennial surveys of education also contain information on the spread of vocational education.

Another way of tracing the changing nature of the vocational movement is through the various periodicals devoted to the subject. See, for example, *Manual Training Magazine, Vocational Education,* and *Industrial Education Magazine.* Educators' viewpoints were expressed in a number of National Society for the Study of Education yearbooks (1905, 1912, 1916, 1924, 1943, and 1965).

The peculiar problems relating to the vocational training of females were frequently touched upon in the general discussions of vocational education. A number of studies, however, specially focused on the subject. Of particular interest were those sponsored by the Women's

Educational and Industrial Union under the general title "Studies in the Economic Relations of Women."

The various approaches to the vocational education of blacks is best developed in August Meier, *Negro Thought in America 1880–1915* (Ann Arbor, 1966) and Henry A. Bullock, *A History of Negro Education in the South* (Cambridge, 1967), though neither of these should substitute for the writings of Booker T. Washington and W. E. B. DuBois.

From its inception, the vocational education movement has been open to criticism and conflict. A major critique is Paul H. Douglas, *American Apprenticeship and Industrial Education* (New York, 1921). George S. Counts, *The Selective Character of American Secondary Education* (Chicago, 1922) provides information on the impact of vocationalism within the framework of more general criticism of American education. The controversy in Chicago over vocational schooling as part of larger social and political conflicts is brilliantly portrayed in George S. Count's *School and Society in Chicago* (New York, 1928). Arthur G. Wirth, *Education in the Technological Society: The Vocational–Liberal Studies Controversy in the Early Twentieth Century* (Scranton, 1972) provides a solid assessment of Dewey's approach to education and technological change and specifically the nature of his opposition to vocationalism in the schools. The best description of the impact of vocational education on schooling, however, is that presented by Robert and Helen Lynd in *Middletown* (New York, 1929).

The first major review of vocational education was that of the Advisory Commission on Vocational Education, established in 1936; the most informative of the resulting reports was published as John Russell and Associates, *Vocational Education* (Washington, D.C., 1938). Almost all of the literature from that time until the early 1960's was concerned with the implementation and the continuing justification of vocational training along previously established lines.

The report of the Panel of Consultants on Vocational Education, *Education for a Changing World of Work* (Washington, D.C., 1963), and that of the Advisory Commission on Vocational Education, *Vocational Education: The Bridge Between Man and His Work* (Washington, D.C., 1968), contain the most influential recent criticisms of vocational training, along with the proposals for a reorientation which formed the basis for the Vocational Education Act of 1963 and the Vocational Education Amendments of 1968. Douglas E. Kliever, *Vocational Education Act of 1963: A Case Study in Legislation* (Washington, D.C., 1965) examines the Congressional struggle. James B. Conant, *Slums and Suburbs* (New York, 1961) was an important statement calling for more effective job training for the urban poor. General evaluations and summaries of recent literature can be found in Jacob V. Kaufman, "The Role of Vocational Education in the Transition from School to Work," in Arnold Weber, Frank Cassell, and Woodrow Ginsberg (eds.), *Public-Private Manpower Policies* (Madison, 1969); J. Kenneth Little, *Review and Synthesis on the Placement and Follow-up of Vocational Education Students* (Columbus, 1970); and Garth Mangum, *Reorienting Vocational Education* (Ann Arbor, 1968). More recent publications of interest include Carl J. Schaefer and Jacob J. Kaufman, *New Directions for Vocational Education* (Lexington, Massachusetts, 1971), and Gerald G. Somers and J. Kenneth Little (eds.), *Vocational Education: Today and Tomorrow* (Madison, 1971).

1

The Manual Element in Education
JOHN D. RUNKLE
(1878)

*This plea for manual training by the President of the
Massachusetts Institute of Technology attracted nation-
wide attention. Its stress on the changes brought by industrialism and the needs to adapt the schools to more
practical ends became common themes in American education by the end of the century.*

There is a growing interest in this subject. The question
is, whether we can introduce the manual element into
our system of public instruction, in order that a larger
number of those whose education, as pupils, ends in the
public schools, shall be led more directly than is now
the case to some specific pursuit. In this direction, it
seems to me, we are to look for the means to elevate and
dignify the labor of our country. We must educate, and
at the same time make skilful, the laborer. In this way
only shall we ever solve this vital problem of the relation
between labor and capital, and, at the same time, most
effectively develop our great and growing industries. . . .

In the early days of the Republic, when our system
of public education was still in its infancy, mental and
manual education were much more intimately connected
than at the present day. The industries of the country
were still in a crude state; agriculture and a few only of

SOURCE: Massachusetts State Board of Education, *Forty-First Annual Report of the Board Together with the Annual Report of the
Secretary of the Board* (Boston, 1878), pp. 185–188.

the more necessary mechanic trades having any existence. These trades demanded but little artistic taste, and not the highest manual skill. But the educational needs of the time were quite well met in the apprenticeship system, which existed then in its best form. The master became responsible, in an important sense, for the mental and moral well-being of the apprentice, besides teaching him the manual of his trade, with such knowledge of the theory, and such experience, as he was able to impart. By his attendance, for three or four months of each year during his apprenticeship, upon the district school, the mental culture of the apprentice was not entirely discontinued; and thus by alternating between the school and the shop, his mental and manual education were never entirely divorced, but each in an important sense aided the other. . . .

As time passed, a more marked separation between mental and manual education began to take place. The schools gradually improved. Better methods of teaching and a larger number of subjects were introduced, and a higher standard set, all demanding more time from the pupil. But quite as marked a change was going on in the industries. Increased demand led to competition, to the invention of special tools to cheapen production, to a greater subdivision of labor, and to the concentration of the individual upon a very narrow range of work. Thus the apprenticeship system for learning a trade in its old and best form has passed away, never to return. As it exists to-day it is an advantage to neither party. The apprentice can only learn a narrow specialty, so narrow, as a rule, that its only value to him is the meagre pittance which he can earn from day to day, but at the sacrifice of any further educational advantages; while the master finds it for his interest to pay for the skill he needs, rather than put into his carefully adjusted chain of operations a weak and nearly useless link. In this way the school and the shop have become so widely separated, that they are no longer mutual helps, as in past times, in developing the highest capacity or the highest manhood. The student who enters the shop at fifteen for a three or four years' apprenticeship seldom returns to the school; and, on the other hand, the student who completes his high-school course at eighteen seldom willingly enters the shop as an apprentice, with the intention of becoming a skilled mechanic, and earning a livelihood by manual labor. His twelve or fourteen years of mental school-work, whether highly successful or not, have, through habit, if in no other way, unfitted him for all manual work, even if he has not in many ways been taught to despise such labor. Thus it happens, that to-day, educators, lawmakers, philanthropists, and all interested in the highest good of the largest number of the people, or in the best development of our growing and varied industries, are looking for the remedy through education, not of the head alone, but of the head and hand combined in the same system, in order that the education may lead each pupil to some definite end, or directly to the threshold of some special pursuit; that the student's skill of head and hand combined shall have some small commercial value when he has completed his prescribed course of study.

There is a growing feeling that our public education should touch practical life in a larger number of points; that it should better fit all for that sphere in life in which they are destined to find their highest happiness and well-being. It is not meant by this that our education should be lowered mentally, but that it should be based, if possible, upon those elements which may serve the double purpose of a mental culture and discipline,—a development of the capacity of the individual with and through the acquisition of artistic taste and manual skill in the graphic and mechanic arts which most largely apply in our industries. It is true that our system of public education aims to prepare those who wish it for further literary and professional study; but for the large proportion of pupils, the Grammar and High Schools are finishing schools; and it would seem not only proper, but just, that they should be adapted to the wants of the largest number. . . .

2

The Fruits of Manual Training
CALVIN M. WOODWARD
(1883)

The most influential proponent of manual education, Woodward initially focused on hand learning's utility in the training of engineers. He soon enlarged his conception, however, to advocate manual training's benefits for all.

. . . I advocate manual training for all children as an element in general education. I care little what tools are used, so long as proper habits (morals) are formed, and provided the windows of the mind are kept open toward the world of *things* and *forces,* physical as well as spiritual.

We do not wish or propose to neglect or underrate literary and scientific culture; we strive to include all the

SOURCE: *The Manual Training School* (Boston, 1887), pp. 202–212. An address originally given before the National Teachers Association in July, 1883.

elements in just proportion. When the manual elements which are essential to a liberal education are universally accepted and incorporated into American schools, the word "manual" may very properly be dropped.

I use the word "liberal" in its strict sense of "free." No education can be "free" which leaves the child no choice, or which gives a bias against any honorable occupation; which walls up the avenues of approach to any vocation requiring intelligence and skill. A truly liberal education educates equally for all spheres of usefulness; it furnishes the broad foundation on which to build the superstructure of a happy, useful, and successful life. To be sure, this claim has been made for the old education, but the claim is not allowed. . . .

I claim as the fruits of manual training, when combined, as it always should be, with generous mental and moral training, the following:—

1. Larger classes of boys in the grammar and high schools; 2. Better intellectual development; 3. A more wholesome moral education; 4. Sounder judgments of men and things, and of living issues; 5. Better choice of occupations; 6. A higher degree of material success, individual and social; 7. The elevation of many of the occupations from the realm of brute, unintelligent labor, to positions requiring and rewarding cultivation and skill; 8. The solution of "labor" problems. I shall touch briefly on each of these points.

1. Boys Will Stay in School Longer Than They Do Now. Every one knows how classes of boys diminish as they approach and pass through the high school. The deserters scale the walls and break for the shelter of active life. The drill is unattractive, and, so far as they can see, of comparatively little value. There is a wide conviction of the inutility of schooling for the great mass of children beyond the primary grades, and this convic-

tion is not limited to any class or grade of intelligence. Wage-workers we must have, and the graduates of the higher grades are not expected to be wage-workers. According to the report of the president of the Chicago School Board, about one and one-eighth per cent of the boys in the public schools are in the high schools. . . .

From the observed influence of manual training upon boys, and indirectly upon the parents, I am led to claim, that, when the last year of the grammar and the high schools includes manual training, they will meet a much wider demand; that the education they afford will be really more valuable; and, consequently, that the attendance of boys will be more than doubled. Add the manual elements, with their freshness and variety, their delightful shop exercises, their healthy intellectual and moral atmosphere, and the living reality of their work, and *the boys will stay in school.* Such a result would be an unmixed good. I have seen boys doing well in a manual training school who could not have been forced to attend an ordinary school. . . .

2. BETTER INTELLECTUAL DEVELOPMENT. . . . Intellectual growth is not to be gauged by the length or number of the daily recitations. I firmly believe that in most of our schools there is too much sameness and monotony, too much intellectual weariness and consequent torpor. Hence, if we abridge somewhat the hours given to books, and introduce exercises of a widely different character, the result is a positive intellectual gain. . . .

3. A MORE WHOLESOME MORAL EDUCATION. The finest fruit of education is character; and the more complete and symmetrical, the more perfectly balanced the education, the choicer the fruit.

To begin with, I have noted the good effect of *occupation.* The program of a manual training school has something to interest and inspire every boy. The daily session is six full hours, but I have never found it too long. The school is not a bore; and holidays, except for the name of the thing, are unpopular. I have been forced to make strict rules to prevent the boys from crowding into the shops and drawing rooms on Saturdays and after school hours. There is little tendency, therefore, to stroll about, looking for excitement. The exercises of the day fill the mind with thoughts pleasant and profitable, at home and at night. A boy's natural passion for handling, fixing, and making things is systematically guided into channels instructive and useful, as parents freely relate. . . .

4. SOUNDER JUDGMENTS OF MEN AND THINGS. The proverbially poor judgments of scholars have led to the popular belief that theory is one thing and practice a very different thing; that theoretically a thing is one way, practically another. The truth is, that correct theory and practice agree perfectly. If in his theory one leaves out a single element of the problem, or fails to give each its due weight, his theory is false. The school-men have been so accustomed to living in an ideal world, the world of books and books only, where they have found only ideal problems, and they have been so ignorant of the real world and the conditions of real problems, that their solutions have very generally been false. . . .

5. BETTER CHOICE OF OCCUPATIONS. This point is one of the greatest importance, for out of it are the issues of life. An error here is often fatal. But to choose without knowledge is to draw as in a lottery; and when boys know neither themselves nor the world they are to live in, and when parents do not know their own children, it is more than an even chance that the square plug will get into the round hole.

Parents often complain to me that their sons who have

been to school all their lives have no choice of occupation, or that they choose to be accountants or clerks, instead of manufacturers or mechanics. These complaints are invariably unreasonable; for how can one choose at all, or wisely, when he knows so little! . . .

I confidently believe that the development of the manual elements in school will prevent those serious errors in the choice of a vocation which too often wreck the fondest hopes. It is not assumed that every boy who enters a manual training school is to be a mechanic; his training leaves him *free*. No pupils were ever more unprejudiced, better prepared to look below the surface, less the victims of a false gentility. Some find that they have no taste for manual arts, and will turn into other paths,—law, medicine, or literature. Great facility in the acquisition and use of language is often accompanied by a lack of either mechanical interest or power. When such a bias is discovered, the lad should unquestionably be sent to his grammar and dictionary rather than to the laboratory or draughting-room. On the other hand, decided aptitude for handicrafts is not unfrequently coupled with a strong aversion to, and unfitness for, abstract and theoretical investigations, and especially for committing to memory. . . .

6. MATERIAL SUCCESS FOR THE INDIVIDUAL AND FOR THE COMMUNITY. Material success ought not to be the chief object in life, tho it may be sought with honor, and worthily won; in fact, success would appear to be inevitable to one who possesses health and good judgment, and who, having chosen his occupation wisely, follows it faithfully. This point might, then, be granted as a corollary to those already given and without further argument.

Our graduates have been out of school less than a year, but I have seen enough to justify me in saying that their chances of material success are unusually good. As workmen, they will soon step to the front. As employers and manufacturers, they will be self-directing and efficient inspectors; they will be little exposed to the wiles of incompetent workmen. . . .

7. THE ELEVATION OF MANUAL OCCUPATIONS FROM THE REALM OF BRUTE, UNINTELLIGENT LABOR TO A POSITION REQUIRING AND REWARDING CULTIVATION AND SKILL. A brute can exert brute strength: to man alone is it given to invent and use tools. Man subdues Nature and develops art through the instrumentality of tools. To turn a crank, or to carry a hod, one needs only muscular power. But to devise and build the light engine, which, under the direction of a single intelligent master-spirit, shall lift the burden of a hundred men, requires a high degree of intelligence and manual skill. So the hewers of wood and the drawers of water are in this age of invention replaced by saw and planing mills and water-works requiring some of the most elaborate embodiments of thought and skill. . . .

Here is where the influence of manual training will be most beneficial. It will bring into the manual occupations a new element, a fairly educated class, which will greatly increase their value, at the same time that it gives them new dignity.

8. THE SOLUTION OF LABOR PROBLEMS. Finally, I claim that the manual training school furnishes the solution of the problem of labor *vs.* capital. The new education will give more complete development, versatility, and adaptability to circumstance. No liberally trained workman can be a slave to a method, or depend upon the demand for a particular article or kind of labor. It is only the uneducated, unintelligent mechanic who suffers from the invention of a new tool. The thoroughly trained mechanic enjoys the extraordinary advantage of being

able, like the well-taught mathematician, to apply his skill to every problem; with every new tool and new process he rises to new usefulness and worth.

The leaders of mobs are not illiterate, but they are narrow, the victims of a one-sided education; and their followers are the victims of a double one-sidedness. Give them a liberal training, and you emancipate them alike from the tyranny of unworthy leaders and the slavery of a vocation. The sense of hardship and wrong will never come, and bloody riots will cease, when workingmen shall have such intellectual, mechanical, and moral culture, that new tools, new processes, and new machines will only furnish opportunities for more culture, and add new dignity and respect to their calling.

3

Extracts from Address Delivered
at Fisk University

Booker T. Washington

(1895)

*The following excerpt reflects Washington's belief that
the future of his race lay in pursuing manual occupations in the South and in receiving an education that
would inculcate the values of hard work.*

I believe that we are going to reach our highest development largely along the lines of scientific and industrial
education. For the last fifty years education has tended
in one direction, the cementing of mind to matter.

Most people have the idea that industrial education
is opposed to literary training, opposed to the highest
development. I want to correct this error. I would choose
the college graduate to receive industrial education. The
more mind the subject has, the more satisfactory would
be the results in industrial education. It requires as
strong a mind to build a Corliss engine as it does to
write a Greek grammar. Without industrial education,
we are in danger of getting too many "smart men" scat-
tered through the South. A young colored man in a certain town was pointed out to me as being exceedingly
smart, and I have heard of him as being exceedingly
smart and accomplished. Upon inquiry, however, I

SOURCE: *Selected Speeches of Booker T. Washington,* edited by
E. Davidson Washington (Garden City, 1932), pp. 37–41.

learned the young man applied his knowledge and training to no earthly good. He was just a "smart man," that was all.

As a race there are two things we must learn to do—one is to put brains and skill into the common occupations of life, and the other is to dignify common labor. If we do not, we cannot hold our own as a race. Ninety per cent of any race on the globe earns its living at the common occupations of life, and the Negro can be no exception to this rule. . . .

I have been told that the young colored man is cramped, and that after he gets his education there are few chances to use it. I have little patience with such arguments. The idea has been too prevalent that the educated colored man must either teach, preach, be a clerk, or follow some profession. The educated colored men must, more and more, go to the farms, into the trades, start brick yards, sawmills, factories, open coal mines; in short, apply their education to conquering the forces of nature.

One trouble with the average Negro is that he is always hungry, and it is impossible to make progress along educational, moral, or religious lines while in that condition. It is a hard matter to make a Christian out of a hungry man. It has often been contended that the Negro needed no industrial education, because he already knew too well how to work. There never was a greater mistake.

I fear that the Negro race lays too much stress on its grievances and not enough on its opportunities. While many wrongs have been perpetrated upon us in the South, still it is recognized by all colored people that the black man has far better opportunity to rise in his business in the South than in the North. While he might not be permitted to ride in the first-class car in the South, he was not allowed to help build that first-class car in the North. He could sooner conquer Southern prejudice than Northern competition. When it comes to business, pure and simple, the black man in the South is put on the same footing with the white man, and here is the Negro's opportunity. The black man could always find a purchaser for his wares among the whites.

4

Report

MASSACHUSETTS COMMISSION ON INDUSTRIAL AND

TECHNICAL EDUCATION

(1906)

The Douglas Commission criticized existing manual training programs and called for a more industrially-oriented educational system. The Commission's most controversial proposal, however, was for the establishment of public trade schools independent of the existing educational system.

From these [statewide] hearings the Commission gained several very distinct impressions regarding matters included in the scope of its investigation.

1. There is a widespread interest in the general subject of industrial education, or special training for vocations. This interest shows itself in two distinct forms, as manifested by two classes of people. There is, first, a general and theoretical interest felt by students of social phenomena and by expert students of education; and, second, a more practical and specific interest felt by

SOURCE: (Boston, 1906), pp. 3–7, 14, 17–20, 23.

manufacturers and wage earners. Men and women who have been brought into intimate contact with the harder side of life as it appears among the poorer people in the cities, who are grappling with the variety of problems of childhood to which city life gives rise, think they see in some form of industrial education a means of securing earlier and greater efficiency as wage earners, more self-reliance and self-respect, steadier habits of industry and frugality, and through these the opening of avenues to better industrial and social conditions.

The broader-minded students of education, men who look at their own work in the light of all its relations to society and to individuals, are coming more and more to feel that education is more than schooling of the old-fashioned type; and that for the fullest development of a child he must early and continuously be regarded as a member of the whole community, must be familiar with all its activities, and must be taught progressively to share in those activities, giving as well as receiving, producing as well as consuming, doing as well as learning. They see that this sort of training is used in the education of the feeble-minded, in the reformation of wayward and vicious children at reform and truant schools, and that it is being used to elevate the colored race in the south; and they ask why it may not be equally efficient in stimulating and directing the higher orders of mind, in preventing as well as curing juvenile delinquency, and in improving the social conditions of white as well as black children.

2. The hearings showed that, besides this general and theoretical interest, there is a practical and specific interest among manufacturers and wage earners because of a *personal need*.

The Commission was told at almost every hearing that in many industries the processes of manufacture and construction are made more difficult and more expensive by a lack of skilled workmen. This lack is not chiefly a want of manual dexterity, though such a want is common, but a want of what may be called *industrial intelligence*. By this is meant mental power to see beyond the task which occupies the hands for the moment to the operations which have preceded and to those which will follow it,—power to take in the whole process, knowledge of materials, ideas of cost, ideas of organization, business sense, and a conscience which recognizes obligations. Such intelligence is always discontented, not with its conditions but with its own limitations, and is wise enough to see that the more it has to give the more it will receive.

Manufacturers confidently believe that a system of industrial education wisely planned would tend to develop such intelligence, while it increased technical skill. . . .

3. The Commission was made aware of a growing feeling of inadequacy of the existing public school system to meet fully the need of modern industrial and social conditions. The opinion was expressed by many speakers that the schools are too exclusively literary in their spirit, scope and methods. Where there was not a pronounced opinion, there was a vague feeling of dissatisfaction with results. This does not imply hostility. Everywhere the Commission found the people loyal to the purpose of the schools, and proud of the advanced position which the State has held, and they do not complain of the cost. They hesitate to criticise, and are far from desiring any revolutionary change; but they are inquiring with open minds whether some modifications may not be possible, by which the schools may reach in a more practical way the great body of children and youth. . . .

5. The Commission early became aware that its pur-

pose and work encountered the suspicion and hostility of many of the labor unions of the State. This was expressed by individual members and by accredited representatives, and was evidently due to misapprehension. It was suspected that the Commission was created to formulate a plan for trade schools supported at public expense. The opposition to such schools is based on the fear that they would furnish workmen in numbers sufficiently large to affect the labor market, and bring about a lowering of wages. These schools are also opposed on the ground that they might furnish workmen ready to take the place of union men during the existence of a strike. "Scab hatcheries" is the significant term by which such schools are characterized. To such schools the labor unions declare themselves totally and unalterably opposed. . . .

MANUAL TRAINING

While the general public has been strangely blind to the narrowness of the public school education, a few people more discerning have undertaken to restore in a measure the balance between manual and mental training which the old-time systems afforded. . . .

The wide indifference to manual training as a school subject may be due to the narrow view which has prevailed among its chief advocates. It has been urged as a cultural subject mainly useful as a stimulus to other forms of intellectual effort,—a sort of mustard relish, an appetizer,—to be conducted without reference to any industrial end. It has been severed from real life as completely as have the other school activities. Thus it has come about that the overmastering influences of school traditions have brought into subjection both the drawing and the manual work. . . .

CONCLUSIONS

As a result of the public hearings and the special investigations, the Commission has arrived at the following conclusions:—

1. For the great majority of children who leave school to enter employments at the age of fourteen or fifteen, the first three or four years are practically waste years so far as the actual productive value of the child is concerned, and so far as increasing his industrial or productive efficiency. The employments upon which they enter demand so little intelligence and so little manual skill that they are not educative in any sense.

For these children, many of whom now leave school from their own choice at the completion of the seventh grade, further school training of a practical character would be attractive and would be a possibility if it prepared for the industries. Hence any scheme of education which is to increase the child's productive efficiency must consider the child of fourteen.

2. Children who continue in school until sixteen or eighteen, especially if they complete a high school course, are able to enter upon employments of a higher grade, usually in mercantile pursuits, and they are able by reason of greater maturity and better mental training to learn the technique of their employment in a shorter time; but they are wholly lacking in manual skill and in what we have called industrial intelligence. For the purpose of training for efficiency in productive employments the added years which they spend in school are to a considerable extent lost years. . . .

3. The productive industries of the State, including agriculture, manufactures and building, depend mainly upon chance for recruiting their service. . . .

4. This condition tends to increase the cost of production, to limit the output in quantity and to lower the grade in quality. Industries so recruited cannot long compete with similar industries recruited from men who have been technically trained. In the long run that industry, wherever in the world it is located, which combines with general intelligence the broadest technical knowledge and the highest technical skill, will command the markets of the world.

5. The industries of Massachusetts need, in addition to the general intelligence furnished by the public school system and the skill gained in the narrow fields of subdivided labor, a broader training in the principles of the trades and a finer culture in taste as applied to material, workmanship and design. Whatever may be the cost of such training, the failure to furnish it would in the end be more costly.

6. The State needs a wider diffusion of industrial intelligence as a foundation for the highest technical success, and this can only be acquired in connection with the general system of education into which it should enter as an integral part from the beginning.

The latest philosophy of education re-enforces the demands of productive industry by showing that that which fits a child for his place in the world as a producer tends to his own highest development physically, intellectually, and morally.

7. The investigation has shown the increasing necessity for a woman to enter the industrial world for the sake of self-support, and hence that she should be prepared to earn a respectable living wage, and at the same time that the attempt should be made to fit her so that she can and will enter those industries which are most closely allied to the home.

The investigation has shown that that vocation in

which all other vocations have their root, namely, the care of the home, has been overlooked in the modern system of education. In order that the industrial life of the community may be vigorous and progressive, the housekeepers need to be instructed in the laws of sanitation, in the purchase, preparation, and care of food, and in the care of children, that the home may be a home, and not merely a house.

RECOMMENDATIONS

The Commission does not deem it to be a part of its duty under the provisions of the resolve creating it, and in fact it is not in the power of a temporary commission to formulate exhaustive and specific plans for industrial education, but rather to ascertain and exhibit the needs of such education and to point out how the State may make effective its existing policy, and to suggest means for the further industrial development of the State.

There seem to be two lines in which industrial education may be developed,—through the existing public school system, and through independent industrial schools. . . .

The Commission recognizes that there should be no interference with the public school system as it exists by a separate authority having co-ordinate powers with those of the Board of Education, yet it believes that the elements of industrial training, agriculture, domestic and mechanical sciences should be taught in the public schools, and . . . that there should be, in addition to this elementary teaching, distinctive industrial schools separated entirely from the public school system. . . .

5

Report of the Sub-Committee on the Relation of Children to the Industries

SUSAN M. KINGSBURY

(1906)

Published as an appendix to the report of the Massachusetts Douglas Commission, this highly influential study documented the large number of school dropouts and argued that without vocational training these youth were doomed to "dead-end" jobs.

It has been said that the years from fourteen to sixteen are the "wasted years" of the child's life. The application was made to the child who enters upon his industrial career at such an age, and when we find that twenty-five thousand of the children of the State of Massachusetts are at work or idle at those ages, we are led to believe that this is the most important question which faces the educational world to-day.

The State releases the child from its educational authority at fourteen, and the child who is no longer interested in the inactive school life, or who feels the stress of necessity for self-support, is forced to search for an opportunity to fit himself for industrial responsibilities. What awaits him? No schools exist which offer practical training until he is at least sixteen or eighteen, and even then they are few in number and usually at a great distance from the child's home. He must turn to

SOURCE: Massachusetts Commission on Industrial and Technical Education, *Report* (Boston, 1906), pp. 25, 86–92.

the "practical school of life" and seek employment, only to find that the doors of those industries which would afford him an opportunity "to pick up a trade" are not open to him until he is sixteen, or usually eighteen years of age. . . .

4. Who decides whether the child shall leave school? The child. Mother after mother declares, "We wanted him to stay in school." The theory that the parent puts the child to work as soon as he can is not tenable, except for the lower foreign element (and even in Lowell almost as large a percentage of the children of native parents are at work as those of foreign parents). Read with the visitor history after history of the child and of the family, and you will find that the child left school from choice, and that the parents objected. But it is much easier to keep the child in school than to put him back into school, and hence the statement that it is necessary for the child to work is often coupled with the declaration that the parent wanted the child to remain in school. The pathetic moment is not when the child leaves school, but when, having been at work, he is thrown out by "slack times," or "quits work" because he does not like it. He will not return to school, and he cannot find a chance to learn a trade. "What shall we do with him?" is the almost tragic question; and the visitor is equally helpless, since she knows that his chances to enter a desirable trade at fifteen or even sixteen, with a seventh-grade schooling, are few. . . .

6. We have seen . . . that the results of entering the unskilled industries range according to the class of industry. Of what educational value are the years in these occupations? The mill affords a more rapid advance in wages for a year or two, but the maximum is attained in a few years. It holds the boy or girl, once having entered, and does not permit of development or advance-

ment to a desirable occupation, unless accompanied by training.

The low-class factories, such as rubber, confectionery, and paper, afford the girl less wages and less opportunity, although they are perhaps more desirable in influence; but they never lead to anything which means development or growth in the industry itself, nor do they serve as a training for any other industry, while they certainly afford no preparation for home duties.

Department stores and errand positions do not afford a living wage, and offer no opportunity for advancement to one. They are distinctly bad in influence, since the younger employee is so shifting, resulting in instability of character. When the child has reached sixteen or seventeen, he or she must begin again at the bottom.

Sixty-eight per cent of the children who commence work between fourteen and sixteen are subjected to the evil influences of these unskilled industries or are in mills. They have wasted the years as far as industrial development is concerned, and in many cases they have forfeited the chance ever to secure it, because of lack of education. . . .

The most important fact in the consideration of wages is that the child commencing at sixteen overtakes his brother beginning at fourteen in less than two years. That his total income in four years would equal that of his brother for six years we cannot prove, but the slight data at hand so indicates.

9. The tendency is to feel that the employment of children is a great disadvantage. The low-grade industries are taking children less and less; even the woolen mills are employing fewer children than heretofore. The result is that the children are forced more and more into juvenile employments or the lower industries.

Another strong and growing tendency is to demand

experienced help, and to refuse all apprentices and younger help. It is certainly a problem as to where the next generation of skilled workers is to come from. Employer after employer refuses to teach, and union after union limits the number of apprentices. Both seem to say to the boy, "Not wanted here."

10. The result is a third strong tendency,—namely, to approve the teaching of the principles of the trades. This demand for skilled and experienced labor on the part of employers is by no means exaggerated. Our technical colleges have produced superintendents,—captains of industry. There are plenty of "helpers" and "lumpers" and young labor,—the rank and file of the army; but there are no expert journeymen, second hands, foremen. If the employer cannot find the responsible man to whom to entrust the $25 duties, it means the journeyman is not advancing,—is not capable of being advanced.

11. Secondary schools of four classes may be proposed to supply this need. The classical or English high school evidently should not be considered in the problem of preparation for the industrial future, since so few of the advanced students or graduates are to be found in the industrial world. To it belongs the professional and commercial problem. When barely 52 out of 2,437 manual training students are found in mechanical trades, it is apparent that the school in which the manual work is introduced for cultural purposes has not met the demands of the trades. The technical high schools have been seen to fit the child rather for technical colleges or for entrance into trades, in which, as a school, the boy advances to the position of captain of industry. Such schools are certainly professional schools of a technical character. They fit for responsibility, but the training of the hand is not sufficiently practical, according to the report of thirty-six out of forty-nine graduates of one of

our most successful schools of this character. Furthermore, they generally recommend less academic work, such as ancient history. These schools are filled with the better class of children, coming from homes above the average or even the high grade of those whom we find in the industries. The short-course trade schools have proved that they interest the younger child, even for a school day of almost twice the length of the ordinary high school; that they are able to teach the general principles and larger processes of certain allied tools and materials sufficiently well to increase the productive power of the child when it enters a trade. But that the responsibility of the child is not developed is declared to be the weakness of such schools. The employer has discovered by bitter experience that the fourteen to sixteen year old child is physically undeveloped, and irresponsible for any sort of work except the actually unskilled.

The development of policy in the industrial world and the experience of educators shows that the productive power of the child before fourteen is negative, and that it has not the power to handle anything but the simplest processes in the simplest and smallest way; that from fourteen to sixteen he is of productive power only for the large processes of manufacture, or for errand work; but that the child in those years, by teaching, may gain the principles of industrial work, which may be put into practice after sixteen; that, therefore, the training before fourteen should be in the simpler practical lines only; that between fourteen and sixteen it should combine the practical training in specific industries with academic work as applied to the industrial problems, to develop intelligence and responsibility. . . .

6

Report of the Committee on the Place of Industries in Public Education
NATIONAL EDUCATION ASSOCIATION

(1910)

The committee's report was a major statement by leading educators on the status of vocational education, emphasizing the importance of a diversified curriculum for a democratic educational system.

The manual-training "movement" and its successor, the present vigorous industrial-education propaganda, have exercised for more than a quarter of a century a dominant influence in the educational thought of the United States. The early arguments for manual training and the later arguments for industrial education have a singular and significant resemblance. More vital motive for school work, better adaptation of the curriculum to the needs of the rank and file, reduction of school "mortality," and promotion of national industrial efficiency—these are among the more urgent reasons that have been advanced, thruout the entire period, for a more adequate attention to "handwork" as a supplement to, or substitute for, the traditional "headwork" of the schools.

With the abandonment of the theory of "general training" based upon the so-called "faculty psychology" the arguments for manual activities in the school, while retaining much of their original form and phraseology,

SOURCE: *Journal of Proceedings and Addresses*, 1910, pp. 652–773.

have been given more specific application than was at first thought necessary. Not motor training, but specific motor abilities; not accuracy, judgment, and honesty, but keener appreciation of some of the most significant industrial processes; not preparation for life—any life— but preparation for a specific kind of life is now urged by those who are leading in the present demand for industrial education.

Notwithstanding the obvious similarity and direct connection between the early and later attitudes toward handwork and industrial activities, there is, then, a most important distinction between the two points of view. The earlier movement emphasized abstract psychological values; the later places the emphasis upon concrete social values. . . .

In the field of elementary education, then, the continuous and at times strenuous discussion of thirty years has not produced results commensurate with the importance attributed to manual training by its advocates. Notwithstanding much notable advance, due largely to the influence of manual training, toward a more intimate and vital connection between thinking and doing in the school, handwork in the school is still in the main abstract, isolated, impractical, and unsocial in character.

The industrial-education propaganda of the past decade has likewise, in a measure, failed to affect educational practice to the extent that public interest, professional and lay discussion, and legislative provisions might have justified one in expecting. There is doubtless a keener appreciation than ever before of the social need for industrial education; but there has been relatively little advance in the way of detailed working-out of curricula, organization, and procedure for industrial schools of various types. Within the last few years, however, the demand for industrial education has made itself felt even within the field commonly assumed heretofore to be the exclusive territory of elementary education; a few public intermediate schools and trade schools of a distinctly vocational type having come into being. The result of these experiments is being awaited with eager interest.

In the field of secondary education, there is even greater discrepancy between the promise of theory and the reality of practice. There are about one hundred and fifty schools of secondary grade in the country that are classified in the reports of the Commissioner of Education as manual and industrial training schools. Of this number, however, only one-half are reported as giving any attention to the manual arts. Thirty of these are public high schools; most of which devote from five to nine hours a week, and a very few as much as twelve hours a week; but fewer than half of them give as much as one-third of their time to such instruction. With two or three possible exceptions, none of these public high schools may be ranked as technical high schools according to the definition proposed in the present report—the distinctive industrial or vocational purpose being almost uniformly absent. . . .

Briefly summarized, the results of the committee's work may be stated as follows:

1. Industry, as a controlling factor in social progress, has for education a fundamental and permanent significance.

2. Educational standards, applicable in an age of handicraft, presumably need radical change in the present day of complex and highly specialized industrial development.

3. The social aim of education and the psychological needs of childhood alike require that industrial (manual-

constructive) activities form an important part of school occupations.

(a) In the elementary school, such occupations are necessary to provide concreteness of motive and meaning; to insure positive and lasting results for instruction; and to bring about a vital relation between life within the school and life outside.

(b) In intermediate schools, industrial occupations are an important element in the wide range of experience necessary for the proper testing of children's aptitudes as a basis for subsequent choice of specific pursuits either in vocations or in higher schools.

(c) In secondary schools, industrial occupations properly furnish the central and dominant factor in the education of those pupils who make final choice of an industrial vocation. Vocational purpose is the distinguishing mark of the "technical" high school as distinct from the "Manual Training" high school.

4. The differences among children as to aptitudes, interests, economic resources, and prospective careers furnish the basis for a rational as opposed to a merely formal distinction between elementary, secondary, and higher education. . . .

The present report assumes that a democratic community, by its very nature, must accept the obligation of providing every boy and girl with an educational opportunity that shall be not merely free, but enlightening; not merely compulsory, but compelling; not merely expansive, but vitalizing. A system of public education affording such opportunities is absolutely essential to the development of an intelligent, responsive, and efficient citizenship; and this, in turn, furnishes the most secure, if not the only, guarantee of a permanent and triumphant democracy. . . .

We have reached again from the standpoint of the study of the developing nature of the child the issue of specialized vocational training. It is evident that the general training of the earlier years of the elementary school should be what is deemed necessary to all and what introduces those who are to specialize in some form of industry to their work of specific preparation. We have not, however, as yet considered sufficiently the problem of the initial steps in differentiation or specialization. This problem is in our democratic system one among the most difficult and important that we face. It is a question whether the problem of determining what the vocation of the man shall be is not more difficult and exacting than that of preparing him for what has been chosen. The European systems of education, which have not been burdened to such an extent as our own with the ideals of a democracy, have found it easy to engraft vocational instruction upon an elementary system intended only for those destined by birth to some form of industry. In our boasted continuous ladder of schools, where the elementary school leads into the high school and the high school into the college, the introduction of special training in industry has not been so simple. It means differentiation. It has seemed like cutting off from the children who took it the opportunity for such careers as were limited largely to those who had completed the higher course. We have felt that education shall give to all an equal chance to attain any distinction in life. Hence we have clung to a system associated with the training of leaders, even tho such a system may be poorly enough adapted to the education of anyone else.
. . . We may confine ourselves to the crying need for a system of education that shall provide training adequate, in the first place, to enable a fairly intelligent choice of a calling to be made and, in the second place,

to prepare for whatever may be selected. We are fully alive to the need for the second of these advances. It is doubtful whether our educational leaders have been in general adequately impressed with the need for a system of school work the primary purpose of which should be to enable the pupil to find himself and the teacher to give to him intelligent advice on the matter.

From the point of view of the development of the child, the age at which this process of experimentation toward a calling should be definitely initiated corresponds fairly well with the beginning of the seventh school year. Its external symptom is the high rate of elimination from school at that time, and its internal sign is the unrest, the questioning of values, the beginnings of "storm and stress" that characterize the commencement of the age of independence, of adolescence. It would seem that at this time the secondary phase of education should begin.

. . . It is possible, however, to distinguish three well-marked functions of education, which might be assigned to elementary, secondary, and higher education, respectively, without much destructive readjustment of our present system. Elementary education concerns the essentials and the fundamentals. It is the education that precedes any attempt at differentiation. With the development of the child up into the age where such differentiation becomes necessary an epoch of experimentation sets in. The main purpose of the education of this period should be to afford an adequate basis of experience for the choice of a specialty and to guide the process of selection. Such education we may call secondary. When once it has been determined as well as is practically possible what the child should do, the time for higher education, that is, for the special preparation for a vocation, has appeared.

On this plan we should not have a system in which, while elementary education is supposed to be for all, secondary education is only for a few, and higher education for the very few; but each phase of the work would find representation in the education of all or most pupils. At the beginning of the seventh grade the work of experimentation might well begin. A large number of children have by this time demonstrated their unfitness for what might be called a professional career. For them the severer studies, involving the power of mind to grasp and utilize the abstract ideas and processes involved in mathematics, science, language, etc., are not profitable. They should be given experimental work along the line of industrial training supplemented by concrete cultural work in literature, civics, geography, and science, such as adapts them for the duties of citizenship and social life. We may tentatively suggest that two years of such work would put these children in the position of making an intelligent choice of a vocational school in which to complete their education.

At the beginning of the seventh school year those whose mental traits make it desirable might enter schools where the older type of secondary work is prominent. But we might expect that continually new revelations will be made in regard to the talents of such pupils, and that little by little those who are unable to do the work that leads to the higher professions will be selected out to enter vocational schools that prepare primarily for intermediate positions in industry, commerce, the civil service, etc. . . .

7

Reports of the Committee
on Industrial Education

NATIONAL ASSOCIATION OF MANUFACTURERS

(1905, 1912)

These two reports set out the Association's major pre-occupations—anti-unionism, foreign competition, and more efficient use of resources—and tie them to its support for vocational training.

[1905]

The question of the right education for the American youth is second only in importance to his having an education at all. Eighty per cent of our public school pupils drop out of the schools before attaining to the high school, and ninety-seven per cent of all our public school pupils, from the primary grades to the high schools, drop out before graduation from the high school. Out of 16,255,093 pupils enrolled in the schools of the whole country only 165,000 are students in the colleges or high schools; only one in one hundred has the benefit of a higher training. We must never lose sight of the fact that the large majority of the working people of all nations are poor, and because of their poverty they are forced to begin the battle of life at an early age. The need of the hour is that something be done for the children of this great and worthy class. Formerly the apprenticeship

SOURCE: *Proceedings of the Tenth Annual Convention* (1905), pp. 142–145 and *Proceedings of the Seventeenth Annual Convention* (1912), pp. 151–161.

system offered to the American boy the opportunity to learn a trade, but to-day the changing industrial conditions, and the bitter and cruel opposition of organized labor as a whole, have nearly destroyed this former safeguard of opportunity. We weigh the meaning of our words when we say that this outrageous antagonism of organized labor to the apprenticeship system constitutes in itself a crime against the youth of the whole nation. The American Federation of Labor in this respect has been and is now the meanest and most cruel of all trusts. *The right of every individual, whether native or foreign born, to learn and earn what he can should be as free as the air we breathe.* It is his natural and inalienable right, and only in free America is such a right denied. Even the youth of the Empire of the Czar are free to learn a trade. It is only in our own country that this conscienceless labor trust has outraged the principles of the Declaration of Independence. Let there be no mistake about this. With the exception of the railway brotherhoods organized labor as a whole is uncompromising in its opposition to the trade school, the apprenticeship system and the open shop; they all involve restrictions on their attempted monopoly. But without this unaccountable antagonism there is the utmost necessity for the establishment of a system of trade schools that will take the place, in part at least, of our almost lost apprenticeship system with their newer and perhaps larger and brighter opportunities. And they will be established more and more generally in spite of everything.

Present and Future Trade Schools

The present technical and manual training schools should receive our fullest endorsement. But these schools do not reach the great class of the American youth most in need of technical or industrial education. To authorize and found and organize trade schools in which the youth of our land may be taught the practical and technical knowledge of a trade is the most important issue before the American people to-day. It is this way only that we can undo the monstrous crime which organized labor has committed against its own people. In none of the professions or of the higher callings of labor is there any attempt made to limit the number of people who may desire to engage in them. It is only in skilled and manual labor that the attempt is made to monopolize the opportunity of life, liberty and the acquisition of property. The organized labor trust has tried to monopolize the opportunity to live. . . .

The absurd doctrine that we as a nation can have too many skilled mechanics or that the American youth can be too well educated in his trade or calling, is as we say, unaccountable. It ought to be recognized as a scientific truth that the higher the skill possessed by a mechanic the more valuable is his labor, both to himself and to his employer and the community. The more effective labor becomes, the higher the wages it commands. It is the workingman himself who will receive the greatest reward from the acquirement of trade education. The more mechanical skill we have the greater will be our national and individual wealth and prosperity. To say that we have too much knowledge or too many intelligent workers is like saying that we have too many shoes, too many suits of clothes, or too many of the other good things of life. In 1902 a contracting firm in New York City employed 4,900 skilled mechanics direct from Europe, paying them fifty cents per day above the union rate, because it was impossible to secure such valuable workmen in our greatest industrial center. We should not depend on Europe for our skill; *we must educate our own boys.*

DEMANDED BY THE LAWS OF BUSINESS

Second only in importance to righting a great wrong committed by the organized labor trust against its own class is the economic necessity for trade schools. Professor Huxley has said that technical and trade education for youth is a national necessity, and that the nation that wins success in competition with other nations must train its youth in the arts of production and distribution. Not only should our country as a whole take a deep interest in this mighty problem, but the captains of industry especially, and all the fathers of American boys, should give trade schools and the trade school idea their enthusiastic support. The best thought of the Nation is agreed that in addition to the common school education the youth of our industrial centers should learn a trade or master some craftsmanship. The American boy should be trained in skilled labor, to the end that he may be equipped to take care of himself in honorable employment, and what is equally important, become a useful and honorable citizen of the Republic. That trade education aids enormously in the development of manhood in its best sense all are now conceding. The American boy who has the advantage of a trade school education is better fitted physically and mentally for the battle of life. Thus, he becomes a stronger factor in the citizenship of the nation. . . .

WHY GERMANY'S COMPETITION IS TO BE FEARED

The German technical and trade schools are at once the admiration and fear of all countries. In the world's race for commercial supremacy we must copy and improve upon the German method of education. Germany relies chiefly upon her trained workers for her commercial success and prosperity. She puts no limit on the money to be expended in trade and technical education. The best and universal thought of Germany has every confidence that the returns from such investment have paid, and will pay, enormous dividends. . . .

[1912]

Our Human Capital

There are two kinds of capital in the world. The one we call property. It consists of lands and machinery, of stocks and bonds, etc. This kind of capital we are abundantly developing.

The other kind is human capital—the character, brains and muscle of the people. Professor Fischer, of Yale, at the head of a very able committee, estimates the human capital, the human resources of our country, as of the money value of $250,000,000,000. This capital we have not developed; we have overlooked the whole question of its complete and efficient development. Yet its value in every efficient nation, is five times in money the total value of all other resources combined. We have, then, in developing the physical resources of our country, done the little thing, relatively; it remains now to do the infinitely greater thing, and it remains to the teachers of tomorrow to be of such kind and ability as will be the great creative and administrative force in the doing of this supremely wonderful thing.

The Human Waste Emotionally

The new conception takes thought, not of what our schools do, but of what they fail to do. It is not unappreciative. It may be over-appreciative—over-appreciative of things undone. It is not satisfied with the number of children who are put through our schools and rounded out in the process. With new eyes, it sees the waste and wreckage of the schools—that fifty per cent of all the children of the nation are not educated, a percentage of waste and wreckage inconceivable, and unapproached in any other line of human activity.

Statistics startle. Somehow it has been supposed that the great body of American children are being educated with some sort of completeness. It is now commonly known that one-half of all American childhood leaves school by the end of the sixth grade, at about fourteen years of age, having only learned the three R's, which are not education in any sense, but only the means whereby education may be attained.

These children are, as it were, thrown out of the school windows, midway the course, dazed, uncertain, unhappy, undirected. Those who can consider this situation with the least complacency must be influenced by the belief that their own children will not be of this lost fifty per cent. . . .

The new conception, then, concerns the educational salvation and direction of this fifty per cent of the child life of the nation—the children of today, the adult, controlling responsible life of tomorrow.

ADOLESCENCE

Not only is an infinite mistake committed in the failure to educate, in any sense, more than half the population, but another mistake lies in the loss, except under the criminal statutes, of all control and direction by the State of its youth in the period of adolescence, say from fourteen to seventeen years. This is the critical time of life, when the will asserts itself, the impulses of maturity are felt, and when, as is recognized by all countries educationally more alert, the developing character needs guidance and cries out for it; for the establishments of standards, for interpretation, and for the strengthening and development of judgment. Germany, France, Belgium, Australia and Switzerland save, and infinitely strengthen and develop, the manhood and efficiency of their people, by retaining an educational control through these years.

THE VALUE OF DAILY TOIL

The new conception, after a century, more or less, of riotous and careless thinking, returns to the primal conception of the dignity and of the infinite educational value of labor; of the precious, ordinary, everyday's hard work, which, after all, has made us what we are.

Says Carlyle: "The latest gospel in this world is, 'Know thy work and do it.' All true work is sacred. In all true work, be it but true hand labor, there is something divine." A noted educator, measuring the educational value of the school of hard knocks and the day's work, made an informal census of all the men who are, today, responsible for the greatness of one of our cities, for its present activities, character and prosperity. He found that substantially all of them left school at about twelve years of age and reached his place among those who were greater than the school-bred men by force of that education that comes of the day's work.

. . . It is the heart and purpose of the new system to unite in one these two schools, that the lessons of the day's work for wages and the lessons of the printed page shall be learned conjointly by this fifty per cent who now leave school by the sixth grade. . . .

CONTENTMENT

The new conception requires that the State shall give reasonable contentment and happiness to that half of the citizenship that the school has heretofore abandoned in the sixth grade. The right to "happiness" is not new. It is guaranteed in the Constitution. Said Solomon: "Wherefore, I perceive it is well that a man *rejoice* in his work, for that is his portion."

Joy in work comes of efficiency in work. Not until now has the public conception of the school's duty included that of making efficient in his occupation, and therefore intelligently happy, every worker, by industrial education. . . .

The boys now in the industrial and continuation schools that have sprung up throughout the land, are so happily absorbed in the ordinary industrial pursuits of the classroom, in brick-laying, carpentry and machine work, in constructive effort, that they say: "No, neither football nor running races, but the problems of the daily task."

Today, our factory children look upon a shop too much as upon a jail. There has developed among a considerable part of the adult factory workers a dislike, almost a hate of work; substantially all of our native-born factory workers are the boys who left school in the sixth grade—just grown up. They have had little education except that of the newspapers and the chances of the public platform and the street.

CITIZENSHIP

Industrial education rightly includes courses in "citizenship," meaning thereby, instruction in civics, in social rights and responsibilities. One-half the trouble between employer and employee, between capital and labor, so-called, will disappear when our workers have the education to which they are entitled, and better understand what are their obligations and how to observe them.

In abandoning, educationally, during generations, one-half the growing population in mere childhood, the American State has put itself in real peril. For various reasons, no vital hurt has come, but now, with every citizen fast coming to feel and assert his equal power, it is beyond question that every citizen must be informed, that he may give and take in reason and with understanding. It will not be enough to have good workers; there must be everywhere a high and intelligent standard of citizenship. . . .

THE ECONOMIC SIDE

. . . Industrially, the United States has reached a position which may fairly be called critical. We have, in the past, been exploiting our marvelous wealth of natural resources. We have thought that in converting these resources into money we were really making money by the amount of the growing bank account—a very false conclusion. If a man sells his house and lot for $5,000 he has not made $5,000; he has only converted property into money; he may be the poorer and not the richer by the transaction.

We should act at once because of the stress of foreign competition. We are twenty-five years behind most of the nations that we recognize as competitors. We must come nearer to the level of international competition. As every manufacturing establishment must have a first-class mechanical equipment and management, so also it must have in its workmen skill equal to that of competitors, domestic or foreign. The native ability, the intuitive insight, courage and resourcefulness of American workmen is quite unsurpassed. They are brothers of "the men behind the guns." It is their misfortune that they have not been given by their country that measure of technical instruction that is their due, and are by no means equal in technical skill to the workers of continental Europe. . . .

THREE KINDS OF CHILDREN—
THREE KINDS OF SCHOOLS

Differing as children do from one another, they may, nevertheless, be divided educationally into three great classes:

1. The abstract-minded and imaginative children, who learn readily from the printed page. Most of the children whose ancestors were in the professions and the higher occupations, so-called, are of this class, as well as many from the humbler callings.

2. The concrete, or hand-minded children. Those who can only with extreme difficulty, and then imperfectly, learn from the abstractions of the printed page. These children constitute at least half of all the child life of the nation, being that half who leave our schools by the end of the sixth grade, with substantially no education beyond an imperfect command of reading, writing and arithmetic, and a bit of domestic geography; that is, of the three R's, which, in themselves, are not education in any sense, but only the tools whereby education may be attained in the seventh, eighth and later grades, if at all —all those studies which develop judgment, citizenship and efficiency coming in these higher grades.

3. The great intermediate class, comprising all degrees of efficiency from those who by the narrowest margin fall

short of the requirements of the first class to those whose capabilities just save them from the third class.

There is something of a tendency, even today, while seeing clearly the needs of the first and second classes, to fail to do as well as we easily can by this third, or intermediate class, by the introduction into the grammar schools of highly developed, practical and extended courses of prevocational and manual training. Wherever introduced, these courses have aroused a new interest and made many backward students alert and bright. They have also developed in an unexpected degree an appreciation of the dignity of labor of all kinds, and such moral qualities as diligence, concentration, perseverance and respect. They have also caused many to successfully continue in school who otherwise would leave discouraged, early in the course. . . .

THE CONCRETE OR HAND-MINDED CHILDREN

It is of the concrete, or hand-minded children, being one half of the youth of the land, that our present educational system has been horribly unmindful, uninformed and inconsiderate. Our educators have been so proud of what they were doing with the fifty per cent of the children who stay in school after the sixth grade that they apparently have thought the loss of the other fifty per cent necessary and negligible.

In a just and intelligent educational system no reproach is allowed to attach to the youth whose mind follows the course of the infinite majority of all ages passed in developing through the concrete. Our schools have acted as if the child might as well be an idiot as be concrete-minded. They have been like the old time operators of blast furnaces, who threw away the slag as bothersome and worthless, not knowing that with a little care it would some day be made into cement and better the life of the world. It is a question, however, if our educators have not as often thrown away the steel as the cement.

It is thought by many that these children ought to leave school and go to work. Doubtless many of them should leave the present-day school. The laboring people realize that their boys will never go into the industries unless they go at about fourteen years of age, that being the time when industry beckons and mechanical pursuits are especially attractive. Experience shows that those who stay in school until they are sixteen insist upon the "white collar jobs" and would sooner earn a little in the hack work of an office than have the ofttimes greater opportunities of industry. . . .

CONTINUATION SCHOOLS

For the children who leave school by their fourteenth year, Germany and other continental countries have, and we must have, a comprehensive system of "continuation schools" (wherein the education of the child is "continued").

These continuation schools must be established in every industrial community in our land. There is no other way of completing or making adequate in any sense the education of one-half our children. . . .

Wages must be continued during school hours, that a child may appreciate that his schooling is as important and valuable as his regular employment. The employers owe it to themselves and the country to make this provision. Experience shows that no part of wages brings better return than those paid for the hours in school. It is the experience of some manufacturers that after a little schooling a boy can take hold of a new machine and in

a week or so do three-fourths as much as a grown man,
while a boy without schooling will take a month or two
to do half as much as a man, with a corresponding waste
of materials. . . .

ADMINISTRATION BY PRACTICAL MEN AND EDUCATORS

Continuation and all other industrial schools must be
conducted upon intensely practical lines. To quote again
from Mr. Cooley:

Vocational schools must be administered by practical men
from the vocations, and educators. Without the practical men
they will not keep in touch with actual life conditions; without the educators they will waste the time and strength of the
pupils by ill considered methods of instruction, and will be
dominated too completely by the vocational aim. We require
men and citizens as well as workmen, and we cannot secure
them without the united effort of both the practical men and
the educators.

SEPARATE STATE AND LOCAL BOARDS OF CONTROL

It is advisable that as in Wisconsin, the development
of industrial education be put into the hands of a special
State Board of Industrial Education, and of similar local
boards in the various communities. Some objection has
been made to a separate board, with the possibility of
friction with the other or general State and local boards
of education. It is suggested in reply that the regular
schools boards have never undertaken a special task of
this difficulty or magnitude. They are busy with their
regular duties. . . .

8

Reports of the Committee
on Industrial Education (1910)
and Commission
on Industrial Relations (1915)
AMERICAN FEDERATION OF LABOR

These reports by committees of the A.F. of L. reveal organized labor's ambivalences about the uses to which vocational training could be put and its fear that without incorporation into the public schools, business would dominate vocational education.

[1910]

The problem of industrial education and trade training is made extremely complex by the present system of specialization, and unless great care is exercised the exploitation of boys who desire to enter upon a career as a skilled craftsman is probable.

A proper apprenticeship system which will guarantee to the youth the opportunity of learning his trade as a whole is very much desired.

One of the disadvantages of many apprenticeship systems is that establishments have become so large and with so many departments with their divisions and subdivisions and processes that the time of the boy is fully employed in mastering details of one department to the

SOURCE: Sixty-Second Congress, Second Session, U.S. Senate, *Document No. 936* (1912), pp. 7, 11–19 and American Federation of Labor, *Report of Proceedings*, 1915, pp. 322–323.

exclusion of all other departments. Public industrial schools or schools for trade training should never become so narrow in their scope as to prevent an all around shop training.

The progressive development of all high-grade industries requires skilled workmen, possessing "industrial intelligence"—that is, comprehensive insight into and intelligent interest in their several trades—as well as skill. The present conditions of production are usually unfavorable to the training of such workmen in the shop or factory, and sometimes render such training impossible. All industries, whatever their grade, need more men than are now obtainable, who are capable of acting as foremen, superintendents or managers—men possessing the comprehensive insight, interest, and skill necessary for the organization and direction of a department or a shop. In general, such men, whether workers, foremen, or superintendents, are now developed only by chance, and they are then self-made men, possessing the merits but also the shortcomings of their training. . . .

POINT OF VIEW

. . . In regard to 1—should trade, vocational, technical, and industrial schools be established as a part of the public school system?

We believe that technical and industrial education of the workers in trades and industry, being a public necessity, should not be a private but a public function, conducted by the public, the expense involved at public cost and as part of the public-school system. In order to keep such schools in close touch with the trades and industries, there should be local advisory boards, including representatives of the industries, the employers, and organized labor.

In regard to 2—should private industrial educational institutions be tolerated?

Organized labor's position regarding the injustice of narrow and prescribed training in selected trades by both private and public instructions, and the flooding of the labor market with half-trained mechanics for the purpose of exploitation, is perfectly tenable and the well-founded belief in the viciousness of such practices and the consequent condemnation, is well-nigh unassailable.

In regard to 3—under what conditions and terms should industrial schools, either public or private, be countenanced and supported?

We believe in private initiative, coupled with active cooperation between the school authorities and the trade unions, or private undertakings which are manifestly for the educational advancement of trade-union members.

In regard to 4—under what conditions should the semi-private or the semipublic industrial schools, namely, the so-called cooperative industrial schools, be approved or disapproved?

The problem is divided into two parts as follows:

(a) Public control of cooperative schools.

(b) Private control of cooperative schools.

As to (a) the cooperative-school plan is an attempt to combine training in the processes and practices of trades, in manufacturing or other establishments, with general instruction in a school which includes theory plus academic studies that bear directly on the trade work. The details of such systems vary, but the most popular is the half-time plan. . . .

In the last analysis, industrial education will be measured by intensely practical men of the industrial world, on the basis of skill and intelligence, as developed by these undertakings, to fit the youth of the country for wage-earning occupations. In order to meet this test successfully, apprentices must be trained under real conditions in productive industry, thereby making the co-operative-school plan a necessary feature of our public-school system.

Other reasons why cooperative schools should be a public charge are as follows:

1. Because of the very nature of things, past and present, the general public has confidence in the public-school system.

2. The manufacturer ought not to be expected to run his establishment to teach trades; nor can he be criticized for making "machine specialists" instead of all-around machinists, when one takes into consideration the fact that he is working to accomplish a very definite end; that is, to turn out a product.

3. The public schools should teach the theory of the trade, while the actual practice and processes should be taught in the shop. This method permits of continuous development of capacity and relieves the manufacturer of the expense of the theoretical instruction, and provides a means of weeding out boys who are not adapted to particular trades.

4. By this method the boy, the employer, and the community are benefited. The obligation to provide industrial education of a theoretical nature, therefore, should rest entirely with the public schools.

As to (b)—private control of cooperative schools:

The committee reaffirms its position in condemning any system of public instruction privately controlled, or any scheme of private selection of pupils, and calls attention to the introduction of a plan which is being put into operation in several localities and fostered by manufacturers' associations.

This cooperative scheme is a limited plan for industrial education, carried on between the high school, which engages a teacher for the purpose, one satisfactory to the manufacturers, and a group of the latter who indenture such boys as they desire to have. The idea is, of course, to give a thorough training. But—

(a) The manufacturer is not obliged to take any boys or to keep any boy.

On the other hand, the high school is obliged to educate all duly qualified boys, to give them all that the city provides.

Therefore those who study in such a cooperative course do so on sufferance.

(b) The people have no hand in this plan. No matter how much a father may desire such training for the boy, the city is helpless to do anything, as under this plan the veto power over the boy's right to public industrial education is in the hands of the manufacturer.

(c) The public school must be neutral as to trade unionism. Surely it dare not be hostile. But what is there to restrain one or all the cooperating plants from assuming any attitude, however hostile? They have the right to teach and to foster antiunionism with school-apprenticed boys under them.

(d) A boy who should talk over or agitate for union principles can be instantly deprived of his educational future under this plan; and if his father should be a known union champion, only the good nature of the manufacturer can prevent reprisal in the form of dropping the boy from this course.

(e) The teacher can not help siding with the manufacturers; he can not protest, should he so wish, if they import scabs, strike breakers, or any sworn foes of unions. It is not for the school to say who shall be the fellow workmen of these young student apprentices. If he be a man of principles, he could not take the boys out of such a shop, for they are under bond.

(f) Finally, with a teacher too soft on the side of the manufacturers, we shall see for the first time in a public-school system a spirit new in evil power—a class of schoolboys trained under a thoroughly un-American system of private selection of pupils, based on no public or competitive method, unless the manufacturers so permit.

A system wholly removed from the salutary supervision of the people.

A system which needs no check in prejudicing the favorites of this system against the large excluded class of their schoolfellows, and later against their fellow workmen themselves.

Any scheme of education which depends for its carrying out on a private group, subject to no public control, leaves unsolved the fundamental democratic problem of giving the boys of the country an equal opportunity and the citizens the power to criticize and reform their educational machinery. . . .

In regard to 7—should their instructors be practical men from the ranks of trade occupations, or should they be men who know nothing of the trade itself except its theoretical side?

The committee believes that experience in European countries has shown that academically trained teachers have been dismal failures; notwithstanding this experience, many so-called trade or vocational schools in the United States have, in the recent past, attempted experiments with academically trained teachers with very unsatisfactory or disastrous results.

The teachers of trades and manual vocations must keep up with modern shop practices and processes in establishments which are doing regular productive work; otherwise they will fall far behind and be teachers of obsolete methods and processes. Successful teachers must be men of practical experience, with more than a text-book acquaintance with the industrial world. . . .

In regard to 8—what should be taught under the head of "Industrial education"—the cultural side, the professional side, the mechanical side, or all combined?

The committee believes that the course of instruction in a school giving industrial education should include English, mathematics, physics, chemistry, elementary mechanics, and drawing; the shop instruction for particular trades and for each trade represented; drawing, mathematics, mechanics, physical and biological science applicable to the trade, the history of that trade, and a sound system of economics, including and emphasizing the philosophy of collective bargaining. This, it is believed, will serve to prepare the pupil for more advanced subjects, and, in addition, disclose his capacity for a specific vocation.

In regard to 9—to what extent, if any, should labor headquarters, labor temples, and labor halls be used to further industrial education?

The committee is convinced that there are conspicuous activities throughout the country known as "educational hours" at central labor union meetings, which might well be exemplified to advance and organize a propaganda for industrial education. Such meetings might also be turned into an educational "forum" in the interest or advocacy of membership by trade unionists on both State and municipal educational boards and committees.

In regard to 10—to what extent should "prevocational courses" be encouraged?

For more than a decade the introduction of properly balanced courses in trade training and the enrichment of these courses have embarrassed the advocates of industrial education not a little; in fact, attempts to scientifically analyze processes and practices of the trades have met with resentment on the part of superintendents, supervisors, and foremen of large industrial establishments. The reason for this resentment is that those usually seeking such information are manual-training schoolteachers, unfortunately the greater number of whom are women. Moreover, it is conceded that such teachers have very little sympathy with trades, as such, but look upon manual and trade instruction as a way out of the difficulty of educating the sub-normal pupil. Hence, the objection of those interested in trades or trade education to thrusting upon industry the dull boy. . . .

While we welcome practical courses for those who are to later enter upon specialized vocational and industrial courses, we maintain that "prevocational courses" should be taught by tutors with practical knowledge of the vocations toward which the pupils are to be pointed; in other words, we can not too strongly condemn any attempt to thrust upon school systems courses of instruction which presumes to try out the adaptability of the pupils for particular vocations and which are taught by women teachers with absolutely no practical knowledge of the metal, woodworking and such other trades for which instruction may be offered.

If "prevocational courses" are to be offered in publicly administered schools in an effort to establish a scheme of vocational guidance, then we insist that such courses be given by men tutors, who not only have a practical knowledge of the particular trades, but in addition, teaching experience coupled with an insight into the adaptability and inclination of the pupils for such vocations.

Finally, we favor and advocate increasing the number of men teachers in industrial schools, as well as "prevocational schools" to the end that all practical instruction in trades be given by properly trained teachers who have had in addition to their teaching experience at least four years practical experience at particular trades. . . .

Conclusions

The committee believes that there are pressing educational needs which can at least partly be solved by the introduction of industrial training. At present a very large proportion of the children leave school between the ages of fourteen and sixteen. They change from one occupation to another, having no particular qualification for any vocation, and gain little in efficiency. Industrial education between the ages of fourteen and sixteen ought to awaken a new school interest and help to retain them longer in school; moreover, if industrial training took the children between the ages of fourteen and sixteen, when they are of little value in a business way and at a time when such education as they have received is of advantage to them so far as it goes, but hardly fits them for actual working places, then it would give them the proper training to prepare them to enter some branch of trade or vocational work. At the time our present public-school system came into operation it met the needs of the people; the industries were carried on in the home, and the children were taught the manual arts there; the boy was taught his trade by his father, and the girl and her mother carried on in the home much of the work now performed in the factory. Economic conditions have changed and the schools must change with them. The ranks of skilled labor are being depleted and the work of the trades is being done by unskilled men or semi-skilled machine specialists.

The trade unions have been waiting in vain for twenty-five years for the manual-training schools to furnish

recruits to the "depleted ranks" of skilled labor. It is
time now to take steps to bring back the standard of
efficiency. We want a system which will develop the
labor power of our people so that every worker may
become interested in his work and approach the limits
of human efficiency. Our public-school system of to-day
teaches too much and educates not enough, and fails
entirely to prepare its pupils for productive labor. It
must be changed, and quickly, and the change must be
radical. We can not add a few experiments in trade
training in our larger cities or introduce intense manual
training in manual-training school departments to supplement a Latin and Greek curriculum. Our boys and
girls must leave school thoroughly prepared by industrial
training to do well some kind of productive work. A
healthy community is impossible without the union of
the schoolhouse, the home, and workshop. Modern life
has not yet accommodated itself to the great revolution
of our industrial system. Nothing but a thorough industrial education and understanding of economical interest
of society can lead to the necessary union between labor
and capital and give peace and prosperity to the present
disturbed and suffering industrial world.

We believe that the education of workers in trade or
industry is a public necessity, and that it should not be
a private but a public function, conducted by the public
and the expense involved at public cost.

[1915]

Judged by a careful observation of all opinions and
conclusions agreed to by the American Federation of
Labor on this subject, it is clearly and unmistakably
evident that the American Federation of Labor has and

does approve and favors including the industrial or vocational education into our public school curriculum.

Whilst urgent for industrial education, there is also evident some apprehension that this proposed industrial education may ultimately give way to an attempt on the part of large commercial interest, whereby the opportunities of the workers' children for a general education will be limited, and which will tend to make the workers more submissive and less independent. To prevent this possible menace it is essential that some standard is agreed to by which to judge and determine whether the education fostered tends to a full development of American freedom and of American manhood and womanhood.

We hold the child must be educated not only to adapt itself to his or her particular calling they are to enter later in life, but that they should be educated for leadership as well; that they should have the power of self-direction and of directing others; the powers of administration as well as ability to assume positions of responsibility.

It is not only essential that we should fit our boys and girls for the industries, but it is equally essential to fit the industries for the future employment of our young men and young women.

A careful review of our industrial conditions will provide further evidence that there are many industries which formerly offered the workers opportunities far more than a sustenance or physical existence, which have been divided and subdivided until the vocation itself, in some instances, is becoming a lost art. The ever-increasing specialization in industrial pursuits, due to existing industrial practices, which limit the workers to but one form of automatic work, or confine them to a highly specialized branch of work, is a very serious evil confronting the workers and society to-day. As specialization increases, this evil will logically and proportionately increase unless stringent measures are adopted to prevent the evils of monotonous and automatic work. What good will come in imparting industrial education in our public schools, if our children are permitted to be fastened to a machine, requiring but the repetition of a few muscular motions? Vocational education is not enough; extreme specialization must be abolished. The future industrial life of our children demands that their immature years are spent in a proper physical and mental upbuilding. Then, too, industrial education should not be allowed to co-ordinate itself with any arrangement which will bring trained and experienced workers into any trade without regard to the demand for labor in that particular trade or calling. A proper apportionment of the supply of labor to the demand for labor must be maintained. What good will industrial education serve; what benefit can be derived, if by such teaching we are to produce a greater number of trained and skilled workers than is required or is possible to be employed in the respective trades or callings? Industrial education under such conditions can only increase the existing economic pressure upon the workers. Industrial education must, therefore, be based on a careful survey of industrial conditions and trade requirements, and should meet the needs and requirements of the workers, as well as those of employers and of the industry.

Ever since the establishment of our public school system, there has been a constant and persistent attempt by large commercial interests to control our public system of education, and to do it for their own selfish purpose. These interests have tried time and again to control the courses of preparation and of training our children solely for the purpose of using them in turning out a maximum amount of articles of exchange and commerce at the lowest possible cost to themselves. In substantiation of these assertions we need only reflect upon the effort made a few years ago in Cleveland, Ohio, and more recently in Chicago, Illinois, where the commercial interests succeeded in influencing the respective Boards of Education to adopt rules which denied our public school teachers the freedom of expression and the right of association. To that degree at least, the teaching force of our public schools has been rendered submissive to the will of these commercial interests. These and other manifestations, on the part of the employing and commercial interests to dominate our public schools' affairs, impel your committee to utter a word of caution and to fully advise you that the future of our public schools and the character of teaching our boys and girls, depend largely upon the attitude and exercise of the forces of labor. It is for labor to say whether their children shall receive a real education in our public schools, or whether they are to be turned out as machine made products, fitted only to work and to become part and parcel of a machine instead of human beings with a life of their own, and a right to live that life under rightful living conditions.

Perhaps the most vicious element threatening to divert the movement of industrial education in our public schools from our American ideals of democracy in education, is the continuous effort made by the commercial interests to place industrial education under the direction of a distinctive board of management, separate from the board of administration governing the general education of the children. A division and separation of authority in educational studies, we believe, will establish a division of educational systems in the minds of the school children and their parents, wherein industrial education instead of proving supplementary to our general education, will be looked upon as the main and most important public system of education. Vocational school courses should at all times be under the guidance and control of school authorities having control of the general education of the children. The unit system of administration is best adapted to educating our children properly for their future guidance as citizens and as workers.

9
The Vocational Education of Females
NATIONAL EDUCATION ASSOCIATION
(1910)

The problems of providing a special kind of vocational education that would prepare women for both home and economy are set out in this report to the N.E.A.

The girls in our schools will be the wives and mothers of the next generation and the courses of study should be so laid out that these girls will lead happier and richer lives and will be more successful as the future homemakers of our cities. If the maintenance of a finer order of home is a matter of the deepest concern to every member of the community, it logically follows that the appropriate training of the mother—the homemaker—is essential to the general welfare. We shall be wise, then, to test every plan for the education of women, not merely

SOURCE: National Education Association, "Report of the Committee on the Place of Industries in Public Education," *Journal of Proceedings and Addresses* (1910).

with questions of immediate expediency or of personal advantage, but always with the thought of the larger contribution to the common good, and the higher function which woman can never surrender.

A large class of girls whose elementary education is incomplete, are in imperative need of such industrial education as will enable them to earn a living wage. Thru their self-maintenance, furthermore, the standard of the family life will be immensely advanced.

The aim of the courses for girls is twofold: (1) It is to enable them, thru the right sort of homemaking training, to enter homes of their own, able to assume the most sacred duties with an intelligent preparation, and to perpetuate the type of home that will bring about the highest standard of health and morals. (2) The courses of instruction should also train for work in distinctly feminine occupations. The time is perhaps not far away when every girl will learn some specific kind of remunerative skilled work, just as we expect boys to do. This does not mean that married women will follow a vocation outside of the home, save in exceptional cases. It does mean that girls will generally earn a livelihood in some skilled work during the three, six, or eight years after leaving school and prior to marriage, and will do so for their own and the good of society; that this earning power will raise the standards of living in their parents' families and give the impulse to a higher level when the girls marry and start their own homes; and further, that this possession of skill in remunerative labor will, after marriage, afford protection and support when a family loses its male head.

10

Report

COMMISSION ON NATIONAL AID TO

VOCATIONAL EDUCATION

(1914)

*The most influential document of the vocational educa-
tion movement, the Commission's report drew together
almost all the prevailing arguments for vocational training, using them to justify federal aid. With minor
revisions, the Commission's recommendations were sub-
sequently incorporated into the Smith–Hughes Act of
1917.*

FINDINGS

THE NEED OF VOCATIONAL EDUCATION. While many
different kinds and grades of vocational education will
always be required, the kind most urgently demanded
at the present time is that which will prepare workers
for the more common occupations in which the great
mass of our people find useful employment.

There is a great and crying need of providing vocational education of this character for every part of the
United States—to conserve and develop our resources; to
promote a more productive and prosperous agriculture;
to prevent the waste of human labor; to supplement
apprenticeship; to increase the wage-earning power of
our productive workers; to meet the increasing demand

SOURCE: Sixty-Third Congress, Second Session, U.S. House of
Representatives, *Document No. 1004* (1914), I, 12–13, 18–27, 32–34.

for trained workmen; to offset the increased cost of living. Vocational education is therefore needed as a wise business investment for this Nation, because our national prosperity and happiness are at stake and our position in the markets of the world can not otherwise be maintained.

The social and educational need for vocational training is equally urgent. Widespread vocational training will democratize the education of the country: (1) By recognizing different tastes and abilities and by giving an equal opportunity to all to prepare for their life work; (2) by extending education through part-time and evening instruction to those who are at work in the shop or on the farm. Vocational training will indirectly but positively affect the aims and methods of general education: (1) By developing a better teaching process through which the children who do not respond to book instruction alone may be reached and educated through learning by doing; (2) by introducing into our educational system the aim of utility, to take its place in dignity by the side of culture and to connect education with life by making it purposeful and useful. Industrial and social unrest is due in large measure to a lack of a system of practical education fitting workers for their callings. Higher standards of living are a direct result of the better education which makes workers more efficient, thus increasing their wage-earning capacity.

An overwhelming public sentiment shows the need for vocational education in this country. The testimony in this behalf comes from every class of citizenship, from the educator, the manufacturer, the trades-unionist, the business man, the social worker, and the philanthropist. Every State superintendent of public instruction declared that its rapid extension was required for many different reasons in his State and great national educational, civic, industrial, and commercial organizations, representing more than 12,000,000 people, have repeatedly gone on record as believing that a system of vocational education was absolutely necessary to the future welfare of the nation.

THE NEED OF NATIONAL GRANTS TO THE STATES FOR VOCATIONAL EDUCATION. While recognizing that training for all the different vocations is important and desirable, agricultural and trade and industrial education are most in need of national encouragement at the present time. The best way to aid the States in giving these kinds of vocational training is through grants for the preparation of efficient teachers and grants for the part payment of their salaries.

National grants are required for the salaries and the training of vocational teachers: (1) To help to solve a problem too large to be worked out extensively and permanently save by the whole nation; (2) to help the States, with their widely varying resources, to carry the cost of giving vocational education and thereby to make this education possible in those States and localities already burdened with the task of meeting the requirements of general education; (3) to equalize among the States the large and unequal task of preparing workers whose tendency to move from State to State is making training for a life work a national as well as a State duty; (4) to give interest and prestige in the States to the work of preparing our youth for useful and productive service.

National grants for agricultural, and trade and industrial education are justified: (1) By the urgency of the demand for the effective training of our workers, which the States can not meet in time without Federal encouragement and aid; (2) by the interstate and national character of the problem, due to its nation-wide interest and importance; (3) by abundant precedent, in appropriations by Congress throughout our entire history, for educational purposes, and in cooperation between the Federal Government and the States, where team play was necessary to handling matters that could not be as well handled by the States alone; (4) by the successful results to the Nation as well as to the States of previous grants for educational purposes.

After six years of consideration of the question by Congress and the country an overwhelming public sentiment favors national grants. The favorable opinions given at the hearings and in answer to questions sent out by the commission to educators, employers and employees, and educational, civic, industrial, agricultural, and commercial organizations national in their scope, were practically unanimous. . . .

THERE IS A CRYING ECONOMIC NEED FOR VOCATIONAL EDUCATION

The two great assets of a nation which enter into the production of wealth, whether agricultural or industrial, are natural resources and human labor. The conservation and full utilization of both of these depends upon vocational training.

1. VOCATIONAL TRAINING IS REQUIRED TO CONSERVE AND DEVELOP OUR NATURAL RESOURCES. As the asset of natural resources lessens or falls in the scale, the asset of human labor rises in importance. American agriculture has prospered in the past because it rested upon the basis of the richest soil in the world—a fertility which, with the usual prodigality of this people, has been treated as if it were inexhaustible. This favorable condition itself has delayed for a century too long in the United States the cooperation of the National Government with

the States in the systematic training of the American farmer. Only thoroughgoing agricultural education, making the farmer an intelligent user of the natural wealth with which Providence has blessed us as a people, can restore and preserve our boasted agricultural supremacy. . . .

The American manufacturer has prospered in the past because of four factors:

(a) The abundance and cheapness of raw material.

(b) The inventive genius of this people.

(c) Organizing ability leading to production on a large scale.

(d) A great body of cheap foreign labor of the first generation working its way upward in our midst to civic and industrial worth.

With the opening of new sources of supply in foreign countries, and with the gradual depletion of our own virgin resources in many lines, our advantage from an abundance and cheapness of raw material, at least so far as regards commercial competition, is a decreasing one. We can not continue to draw indefinitely on Europe for cheap labor, nor will cheap labor in the immediate future meet the urgent need in American industry for the more intelligent service necessary if we are to satisfy the rising demand for a better product from our domestic as well as our foreign markets. In the proportion that our resource factor fails we must increase the efficiency of human labor in the shop as well as on the farm. . . .

2. VOCATIONAL TRAINING IS NEEDED TO PREVENT WASTE OF HUMAN LABOR. The greatest treasure which this country holds to-day is the undeveloped skill and vocational possibilities, not only of the millions of our workers everywhere, but of the great army of our school children, hundreds of thousands of whom pass annually from the doors of our elementary schools to serve in the

shop, the field, and the office. So far we have given but little attention to the conservation of our human resources.

Vocational education will reduce to a minimum the waste of labor power, the most destructive form of extravagance of which a people can be guilty. . . .

4. VOCATIONAL TRAINING IS NEEDED TO INCREASE WAGE-EARNING POWER. The practical training of workmen in any pursuit brings both immediate and lasting economic returns in increased production and wage-earning capacity. The returns of our older trade, technical, and apprenticeship schools show that the wage-earning power of their graduates steadily increases as a direct result of their training. For the thoroughly trained worker wages advance from year to year with age and increased capacity with no fixed limit, and while the average increase is large the increase in individual cases is often very large.

5. VOCATIONAL TRAINING IS NEEDED TO MEET THE INCREASING DEMAND FOR TRAINED WORKMEN. With the constantly increasing demand upon our industries for more and better goods, the supply of trained workers is, relatively at least, diminishing. We are already beginning to feel the inevitable economic results in a relatively low output, increased cost of production, and stationary or diminishing wages as measured by their purchasing power. The product of our factories is being restricted in quantity and quality, if not actually diminished. High prices are due in part to inefficient labor and low profits to the same cause. Inaction means the promotion of poverty and low standards of living and a general backwardness in industry. . . .

7. VOCATIONAL EDUCATION IS A WISE BUSINESS INVESTMENT. In the last analysis expenditure of money for vocational education is a wise business investment which will yield larger returns, not only in educational and

social betterment but in money itself, than a similar amount spent for almost any other purpose. The commission recognizes that boys and girls can not be valued in terms of dollars and cents, save as these represent returns in social well-being both to themselves and to society. The financial argument below is offered from that standpoint alone.

There are more than 25,000,000 persons eighteen years of age and over in this country engaged in farming, mining, manufacturing and mechanical pursuits, trade and transportation.

If we assume that a system of vocational education, pursued through the years of the past, would have increased the wage-earning capacity of each of these to the extent of ten cents a day, this would make an increase in wages for the group of $2,500,000 a day, or $750,-000,000 a year, with all that this would mean to the wealth and life of the Nation. This is a very modest estimate, and while no complete figures are available it is probably much nearer twenty-five cents a day, which would make a total increase in wages of $6,250,000 per day and $1,875,000,000 per year. . . .

8. OUR NATIONAL PROSPERITY IS AT STAKE. We have become a great industrial as well as a great agricultural nation. Each year shows a less percentage of our people on the farms and a greater in the cities.

Our factory population is growing apace. Our future as a nation will depend more and more on the success of our industrial life, as well as upon the volume and quality of our agricultural products. It has repeatedly been pointed out that the time is not far distant when our rapidly increasing population will press hard upon an improved agriculture for its food supply, and force our industries to reach out over the entire world for trade wherewith to meet the demands for labor of untold millions of bread winners. . . .

The volume of our foreign trade has in the past depended upon the exploitation of a virgin soil and of our other national resources. In this crude work we have had no competitors. Our profit has been the profit of the miner working in a rich soil. The volume and profitableness of our trade in the future, however, must depend much more largely upon the relative skill and efficiency of the vocationally trained artisans of England, France, and Germany. Our products will find a market in foreign countries only in those lines of industrial activity in which the labor is as efficient and as well trained as the labor of the countries with which we must compete.

The battles of the future between nations will be fought in the markets of the world. That nation will triumph, with all that its success means to the happiness and welfare of its citizenship, which is able to put the greatest amount of skill and brains into what it produces. Our foreign commerce, and to some extent our domestic commerce, are being threatened by the commercial prestige which Germany has won, largely as the result of a policy of training its workers begun by the far-seeing Bismarck almost half a century ago.

France and England, and even far-off Japan, profiting by the schools of the Fatherland, are now establishing national systems of vocational education. In Germany, within the next few years, there will probably be no such thing as an untrained man. In the United States probably not more than 25,000 of the eleven or twelve million workers in manufacturing and mechanical pursuits have had an opportunity to acquire an adequate training for their work in life.

SOCIAL AND EDUCATIONAL NEED FOR VOCATIONAL TRAINING IS EQUALLY URGENT

This conclusion is based on such considerations as the following:

1. VOCATIONAL TRAINING IS NEEDED TO DEMOCRATIZE THE EDUCATION OF THE COUNTRY:

(a) *By recognizing different tastes and abilities and by giving an equal opportunity to all to prepare for their life work.* Equality of opportunity in our present system of education is not afforded to the mass of our children. While our schools are opened freely to every child, their aims and purposes are such that a majority of the children are unable to take advantage of them beyond a certain grade and hence do not secure at public expense a preparation for their work in life. Although here and there we see the beginnings of change, it is still true that the schools are largely planned for the few who prepare for college rather than for the large number who go into industry.

Only half of the children who enter the city elementary schools of the country remain to the final elementary grade, and only one in ten reaches the final year of high school. On the average, ten per cent of the children have left school at thirteen years of age; forty per cent have left by the time they are fourteen; seventy per cent by the time they are fifteen; and eighty-five per cent by the time they are sixteen years of age. On the average the schools carry their pupils as far as the fifth grade, but in some cities great numbers leave below that grade.

If we assume that all children should have a minimum school training equivalent to the eight grades of the elementary school, we must acknowledge that the schools now furnish this minimum to less than half the children who enter them. The rest leave school with inadequate general education and with no special training to fit them for work. Vocational courses are therefore needed to attract and hold in school pupils who now leave because they are unable to obtain suitable preparation for useful employment. For such pupils the vocational courses also offer the only opportunity the schools have to give further training in citizenship.

Our whole scheme of education presupposes leisure to acquire academic culture or to prepare for leadership in the professions. Vocational culture and training for leadership in industry is equally important, and these can come only when education is broadened to meet the needs of all the children; so that each and every one may have a chance to develop in accordance with his or her capacity and be prepared to render to society the particular service of which he or she is capable.

(b) *By extending education through part-time and evening instruction to those who must go to work in the shop or on the farm.* Only a meager percentage of the workers of to-day are trained for their work, and the armies of children going out from school at fourteen and fifteen years of age annually swell the ranks of the untrained. Whether from necessity or not, the economic fact is that the mass of children go to work as soon as the laws of the various States permit. It is not solely because the children and their parents do not appreciate the value of an education that more than half of the entire number who enter the elementary school do not remain to complete it. It is, at least to some extent, because neither they nor their parents are able to see in the schools of to-day an opportunity for education and training to fit for callings which they must pursue. It is for the States and the Nation, not only to see that these children are prepared for life's battles before they leave school, but to supplement their work by after-training in part-time and evening schools, so as to insure them the largest possible opportunity for development in everything that makes for useful and happy citizenship.

The United States is one of the few large nations which does not provide by legislation for the continued education of children who become wage earners at fourteen years of age. The period from fourteen to eighteen years of age is the one in which the youth is finding himself in society and setting up standards which will largely determine his future conduct and career, and it is therefore important to continue his training both for general civic intelligence and for vocational preparation. If allowed to drift during this period, or if placed in an unwholesome or degrading environment, he may fail to realize his own possibilities of development and may become a dependent or injurious member of society. The adolescent period is, therefore, the critical period during which the individual wage earner needs training for citizenship as well as training for work.

2. Vocational Training Is Needed for Its Indirect but Positive Effect on the Aims and Methods of General Education:

(a) *By developing a better teaching process through which children who do not respond to book instruction alone may be reached and educated through learning by doing.* There are many over age children in the grades, many who fail to be promoted from year to year and soon lose interest and drop out of school. Many of these retarded children are present in the few elementary vocational schools already established in this country, and many teachers in these schools have testified to the remarkable progress made by these children under a kind of instruction which is suited to their interests and abilities, which utilizes the experience of the child and relates the instruction to his motor activities. This is the most successful way of teaching the normal child or man.

At the same time it should be pointed out that so far as vocational schools themselves are concerned they are by no means institutions for the primary purpose of dealing with slow or retarded children. These schools are such as to call for the best efforts of study of vigorous and intelligent boys and girls seeking preparation for an important life work.

(b) *By introducing into our educational system the aim of utility to take its place in dignity by the side of culture, and to connect education with life by making it purposeful and useful.* The mission of vocational education is not only to provide definite training in the technique of the various occupations, but to relate that training closely to the science, mathematics, history, geography, and literature which are useful to the man and woman as a worker and a citizen. Under such instruction the student worker becomes familiar with the laws of health and with his rights and obligations as a worker and a citizen in relation to his employer, his fellow employees, his family, the community, the State, and the Nation. By thus relating education closely to the world's experience it becomes purposeful and useful and enables the worker to see the significance of, to use, and to interpret in terms of his own experience, the knowledge and culture which the race has accumulated. Such education is at least entitled to a place in dignity by the side of the more formal and literary culture now given by the schools.

3. INDUSTRIAL AND SOCIAL UNREST IS DUE IN LARGE MEASURE TO A LACK OF VOCATIONAL TRAINING. The absence of opportunity for creative work and, hence, for full self-expression is, without doubt, one of the causes

of much of the present unrest. The tendency of large scale production to subdivide labor almost indefinitely and to confine a worker to one monotonous process, requiring little save purely manipulative skill, while effective so far as the material product is concerned, is serious when measured in terms of human values. It is safe to say that industry in its highly organized form with its intense specialization, is in the main narrowing to the individual worker, and while "hands" alone may satisfy the immediate demands of industry, the failure to recognize and provide for human progress and development is producing a restless and discontented people.

Out of this unrest comes a demand for a more practical education for those who toil, an education that will better fit them to progress in industry and enable them to rise to ranks of leadership and responsibility. Everywhere it is the opinion of those who are studying the conditions of society that the lack of practical education is one of the primary causes of social and industrial discontent.

Evidence such as that presented by bureaus which are struggling with the problem of unemployment emphasize this need. One of these bureaus states that less than three out of fifty men who apply for work have ever had any sort of trade training or apprenticeship. Most of them have been forced to fit into some particular niche of industry as young untrained boys, have been too readily thrown out with the introduction of new inventions or devices, and help to swell the army of the unemployed. A former State pardon attorney has said that "nearly three-fourths of the persons found in our penitentiaries are persons unable to earn a living excepting at the most rudimentary form of labor."

4. HIGHER STANDARDS OF LIVING ARE A DIRECT RESULT OF BETTER EDUCATION. Better standards of living

are in the main dependent upon two important factors —namely, an increased earning capacity for the great mass of our people and a better understanding of values. Vocational education aims at both. Where there is intense poverty there is little hope of developing higher standards. The one hope of increasing the family income lies in better vocational training.

It is equally true that vocational education enlarges the worker's vision and arouses within him a desire for progress. This is shown by the number of men and women who, by means of further training and education, raise themselves from the ranks of unskilled labor to take positions requiring large directive powers and responsibilities. Our only hope of progress is in helping the individual to help himself. This is at the bottom of all social uplift. To educate boys and girls to perform their chosen tasks better; to understand the relation of their particular work to the whole; to know what their labor is worth and demand a proper return for it, and to broaden their horizon so that both their money and their leisure time may be spent for the things that are most worth while—this is the task of vocational education. . . .

5. THE STATES CAN NOT DO THE WORK BY THEMSELVES. Without the aid of national grants extensive vocational education might come in time, but very slowly. After ten years of agitation, many States have not even made beginnings in this direction.

Every Commonwealth is heavily burdened with the task of meeting the new demands in general education which the twentieth century is thrusting upon the school. Restricted mainly to the revenue from a property tax, the States lack the means to cope with the task successfully. They are reluctant to tax themselves for the entire support of expensive forms of practical instruction when they see the trained men and women drifting away to other States and carrying to them rich assets in citizenship and workmanship.

Additional sources of revenue which otherwise would lie open for use by the States are being rapidly taken over by the National Government through such legislation as the income tax and the corporation tax. There are not wanting those who point out the necessity for the National Government to supplement the more limited resources of the taxing power of the States, particularly under conditions just described, by grants for special purposes, such as vocational education.

Local communities all over the land are under a restricted taxing power, on the one hand, and, on the other, under increasing requirements, many of which have been imposed upon them by the State constitutions and laws. As a result, most of them are finding it very difficult to meet their present financial problems. The burden is particularly heavy in the communities that most need agricultural and industrial education—the small country town—and the industrial center where the demands on the taxpayer are increasing. Practical education, when given properly, will be costly as compared with regular education. To give it otherwise is a waste of time and money. Cities and towns and the country places must have aid else they will not attempt the task at all or will do it so poorly, because of their excessive burdens, that it may result in more harm than good.

6. NATIONAL GRANTS ARE JUSTIFIED BY THE INTERSTATE CHARACTER OF THE PROBLEM OF VOCATIONAL EDUCATION, due to the interstate character of our industries and the national character of State business and industrial life. Because of its extreme mobility labor, particularly that which is skilled and is therefore in great de-

mand, has taken on a national character. A man may be born in Indiana, trained as a worker in Massachusetts, and spend his days as a machinist in California. A State can not be expected to devote large sums from her public revenues to the making of good workmen for the benefit of other States. Only out of a common fund like the National Treasury can the burden be equalized and adjusted so that each State may in justice be expected to meet the obligation resting upon its schools. . . .

Although we are a group of sovereign States, each one of whose constitutional rights must be carefully safeguarded, industry, commerce, and labor are so interrelated that the National Government must be the unifying agency through which the States operate. This is recognized as essential in handling all such problems as those relating to national defense, the improvement of rivers and harbors, the postal service, and the making of good roads, whose character is such that they can not be handled properly by individual States alone. This has always been the work of the National Government for which it was established by the Constitution. The proposal that the Nation should undertake to help the States deal with the task of providing vocational training for its millions of workers is only an attempt to extend the same policy to another important endeavor which is interstate in character and is not in any way an attempt to infringe upon the right of a State to control its own educational system.

7. NATIONAL GRANTS FOR VOCATIONAL EDUCATION ARE JUSTIFIED BY THE NATIONAL CHARACTER OF THE PROBLEM, for it concerns all the people and is of nation-wide interest and importance. It is the duty of the National Government, in so far as it does not interfere with the constitutional rights of the States, "to promote the general welfare." National efficiency is the sum total of effi-

ciency of all individual citizens and the national wealth is the sum of their wealth-producing capacity. While, therefore, our national prosperity in the past has been based largely upon the exploitation of our national resources, in the future it must be based more and more upon the development, through vocational education, of our national resource of human labor. In the markets of the world we compete, not as individuals, but as a unit against other nations as units. This makes the protection of our raw material and of our productive skill and human labor a national problem, and unquestionably introduces a national element into vocational education, making the right preparation of the farmer and the mechanic of vital concern to the Nation as a whole. . . .

11

Smith–Hughes Act

U.S. CONGRESS

(1917)

*Following the guidelines of the Commission on National
Aid to Vocational Education, Congress committed itself
to federal financing.*

An Act to provide for the promotion of vocational education; to provide for co-operation with the states in
the promotion of such education in agriculture and the
trades and industries; to provide for co-operation with
the states in the preparation of teachers of vocational
subjects; and to appropriate money and regulate its expenditure.

Be it enacted by the Senate and House of Representatives of the United States of America in Congress as-
sembled: That there is hereby annually appropriated,
out of any money in the Treasury not otherwise appropriated, the sums provided in sections two, three,
and four of this Act, to be paid to the respective states
for the purpose of co-operating with the states in paying the salaries of teachers, supervisors, and directors of
agricultural subjects, and teachers of trade, home economics, and industrial subjects, and in the preparation
of teachers of agricultural, trade, industrial, and home
economics subjects; and the sum provided for in section
seven for the use of the Federal Board for Vocational
Education for the administration of this Act and for the

SOURCE: Sixty-Fourth Congress, Second Session, *Public Acts and
Resolutions*, Public Document No. 347, pp. 929–936.

purpose of making studies, investigations, and reports to aid in the organization and conduct of vocational education. . . .

12
Practical Arts and
Vocational Guidance
CHARLES A. PROSSER
(1913)

Charles A. Prosser, the secretary of the National Society for the Promotion of Industrial Education, elaborates some of the necessities for vocational guidance.

All boys and girls are, in the neighborhood of fourteen years of age, required to make a choice of some kind. They decide first of all whether they are to attend school or go to work. If they are to attend school, they must decide what kind of school they are to enter. As vocational schools, or departments, are established to meet the needs of those who are not destined for business and professional careers, every pupil ought, as the results of his previous training, to be in a position at fourteen years of age to make an intelligent choice of the occupation which he desires to follow or the kind of training which he wishes. This can only be done by some system of instruction, in the upper grades of the elementary schools, which will test pupils out by other things in addition to arithmetic, spelling, reading, writing, and other traditional subjects of a general education.

SOURCE: *Manual Training Magazine* (1913), reprinted in Meyer Bloomfield (ed.), *Readings in Vocational Guidance* (Boston, 1915), pp. 354–356.

The results of our failure through the schools to properly direct and train all the children of all the people for useful service are unmistakable. Misfits in all vocations confront us everywhere. Many workers are inefficient because they are not adapted to the work they are doing, and some because they have not been properly prepared for it. This lack of efficiency constitutes a permanent handicap not only to the worker but to the calling which he follows. It means lessened wage, uncertain employment, failure of promotion, economic struggle, waste in the use of material, poor workmanship, reduced output, and the lowering of the standards of skill and workmanship of American industries.

We talk much to-day of the necessity of conserving our natural resources. Let us not forget that the richest asset which this country possesses is the practical and constructive ability of the children who sit in our schoolhouses to-day, who are to be the workers and the leaders in industry of the future, and whose talent and aptitude, whatever it may be, can only be uncovered by some system of training within the schools that will give it a chance for expression. Every consideration requires that every worker should have a chance to discover and to develop to the full all his possibilities, both for the good of himself and for the welfare of the social order. It is idle for us to talk much about conserving our natural resources, until we have, by a system of vocational guidance and training, developed a type of intelligent skilled workmen in shop and home and farm who will so deal with the products of our soil and our mines as to eliminate waste and transform them into products of higher and still higher value.

Above all, we must in some way secure a better adjustment of every worker to the calling in which he can work most successfully, in order that he may have the joy that comes from a sense of achievement, and experience the uplift that blesses every man who finds himself employed at a task in which he is interested and at which he is able to render a service creditable to himself and beneficial to his fellows.

Vocational guidance and vocational education are necessary in meeting the problem of fitting the great mass of our people for useful employment, each as the handmaiden of the other and each as indispensable to the success of the other. . . .

13
Equality of Educational Opportunity
CHARLES W. ELIOT
(1908)

One profound impact of the vocational education movement was the redefinition of equality of educational opportunity it entailed. This statement by Harvard University President Charles W. Eliot and the one following by Edward C. Elliott, Professor of Education, the University of Wisconsin, argue that schools should be sorting devices, placing youth into differentiated curriculum on the basis of their predicted vocational roles.

But how shall the decision be made that certain children will go into industrial schools, others into the ordinary high schools, and others again into the mechanic arts

SOURCE: "Industrial Education as an Essential Factor in our National Prosperity," National Society for the Promotion of Industrial Education, *Bulletin*, No. 5 (1908), pp. 12–14.

high schools? Where is that decision to be made? It must be a choice, or a selection. Here we come upon a new function for the teachers in our elementary schools, and in my judgment they have no function more important. The teachers of the elementary schools ought to sort the pupils and sort them by their evident or probable destinies. I am afraid that strikes you at once as an undemocratic idea, but let us see whether it is undemocratic or not.

Does democracy mean that all people are alike? Does it mean that all children are equal? We know they are not. Many of us have seen that in the same family, with the same inheritances and the same environments, the children often illustrate an astonishing variety of disposition and capacity. If democracy means to try to make all children equal or all men equal, it means to fight nature, and in that fight democracy is sure to be defeated. There is no such thing among men as equality of natural gifts, of capacity for training, or of intellectual power.

Germany, which is not generally conceived of as a democratic country, and Switzerland, which is a true democracy, have both discovered how to sort their children. It is done by the teachers and parents in combination, with the help of the children, and it is the very best thing that a teacher can do for a child, to tell him or her in what line he or she can have the most successful and the happiest life. We must get rid of the notion that some of us were brought up on, that a Yankee can turn his hand to anything. He cannot in this modern world; he positively cannot.

Of course, the reason for this change in the capacity of the Yankee is that one hundred years ago there did not exist the great variety of complicated occupations based on applied science, with which we are now confronted on every hand. . . .

Here is the teacher's guide in sorting children. Each child must be put at that work which the teacher believes that child can do best. It used to be the way to set children to do the things they could not do well; but that doctrine, I am thankful to say, is now outgrown. We have learned that the best way in education is to find out what the line is in which the child can do best, and then to give him the happiness of achievement in that line. Here we come back to the best definition of democracy.

14

Equality of Educational Opportunity
EDWARD C. ELLIOTT
(1908)

In fact, "equality of educational opportunity" bears every stamp of academic and philosophic abstraction. It never was, nor never will be, an ideal capable of realization. What we have, and shall attempt to bring about thru our public school, is an *equilibrium,* a balancing, of educational opportunity. Equality is significant of similarity, identity, of reward. An equilibrium of opportunity implies that grade of reward commensurate with capacities, whether those capacities are of the endowments of nature, of the acquisitions of training, or of the fullness of family coffers. The maintenance

SOURCE: "Equality of Opportunity Can Be Secured Only By Proper Recognition of (a) Individual Differences in Native Capacities And In Social Environment, (b) The Requirements of Vocational Efficiency As Well As Of (c) General Intelligence and Executive Power," National Education Association, *Journal of Proceedings and Addresses* (1908), pp. 159–161.

of such an equilibrium of educational opportunity will result in giving to industry its rightful share of competence, and give to education for vocation its rightful share of social respectability; neither of which may be said to obtain today. . . .

The chief argument in support of the main proposition that some definite preparation for vocational activity, especially industrial, within our scheme of public education, may be derived from the necessary improvement of the acknowledged selective function of the school. At the present moment, the distinct tendency is toward horizontal stratification of individuals into social classes, instead of a vertical selection according to specific efficiency. Vocational industrial education for all is no more likely to yield larger social results than the traditional, pseudo-cultural, static education of the present, unless it becomes consciously selective, unless it consciously fits the square industrial worker into the square industrial hole, the round worker into the round hole, the triangular worker into the triangular hole.

. . . What is needed today . . . is investigation; facts, "Gradgrindian" facts pertaining to industry and to children. We need to determine, first of all, the extent of the demand for trained workers in specific fields of industry; we need to determine the character and the quality of the specific interest and capacities needed by specific industries. Above all, we need to determine the extent, actual and potential, of the individual possession of these specific interests and capacities. Here opens an entirely new field of activity for the study of social needs, and for the study of the pupils of the public school.

This study of social needs, this evaluation of industrial conditions, can be carried on successfully according to projected plans by a comparatively few trained scientists and skilled investigators. But the study of the individual vocational intelligence and interests, ideals and capacities, motives and necessities of the American boy and girl must be carried on, in the largest measure, by the school. Yet the school dare not assume the responsibility for such study, until there is raised up a new generation of public-school teachers—especially in the elementary schools—who know how to detect, to classify and to direct the potential industrial powers of the child. Even given such teachers, this goal is not possible until we begin to rid ourselves of the factory, piece-work system of education of our graded school. This of itself is an almost sure preventive against knowing very much about any individual pupil. The sum total of the superficial observations of eight or a dozen teachers, each of whom has an opportunity of studying and knowing the child merely thru one-half of a year, or at the most, thru a whole year, will not equal one-tenth part of the insight that a skilled, observant teacher might obtain, did the machinery of the public school permit close contact between pupil and teacher, thru several years.

Until we possess reliable data upon which to base a rational scheme of reorganization, the public schools cannot hope to become instruments for "industrial determination"; neither will they cease to prevent the present positive mis-selection of individuals for their proper station of efficiency and happiness. For a rightful selection must precede and underlie the maintenance of the educational equilibrium of democracy.

15

The Need for Vocational Schools
Edwin G. Cooley
(1912)

A major source of conflict was the extent to which voca-
tional training programs should be segregated from
existing school systems. Here, the former superintendent
of schools in Chicago justifies separate trade schools.

It is plainly impossible to provide in the present system
of elementary and secondary schools the instruction recommended. Separate schools are necessary whose equipment, corps of teachers, and board of administration
must be in the closest possible relation to the occupations. In such schools the applications of general education to vocational work can be made only by men who
know the vocations. The boards of education administering such institutions must give them far greater
attention on the practical side than the ordinary boards
of education need to do in the case of academic schools.
No corps of teachers can be expected to keep up with
all the latest developments in vocational life. This must
be the special problem of the boards of practical men
administering the schools.

These schools must not in any way be regarded as
substitutes for the present forms of schools. The present
system is doing a necessary work, and ought not to be
disturbed, except to perfect it. The new type of school
is a supplement to the old one, an attempt to carry

SOURCE: *Educational Review,* XLIV (1912), 449–450.

further and apply general education to the practical problems of life.

Such a system of schools will require a special tax to support it. The present school revenues are insufficient for the present needs of the schools. No part of this general school revenue should be set aside for the support of a system of vocational schools. A special tax, one-half raised by the community served, and one-half provided in the shape of a state grant when authorized by a Commission on Vocational Education, should be provided for the support of these vocational schools.

Such schools should be separate, independent, compulsory day schools, supported by special taxes, carried on usually in special buildings, administered by special boards of practical men and women, taught by specially trained practical men from the vocations, and securing the closest possible cooperation between the school and the factory, the school and the farm, the school and the counting-room, or the school and the home. Adaptation and cooperation are the watchwords for the new type of schools. . . .

16

An Undemocratic Proposal
John Dewey
(1913)

Dewey was one among many who attacked the idea of segregated vocational programs as being wasteful and class–biased.

No question at present under discussion in education is so fraught with consequences for the future of democracy as the question of industrial education. Its right development will do more to make public education truly democratic than any other one agency now under consideration. Its wrong treatment will as surely accentuate all undemocratic tendencies in our present situation, by fostering and strengthening class divisions in school and out. It is better to suffer a while longer from the ills of our present lack of system till the truly democratic lines of advance become apparent, rather than separate industrial education sharply from general education, and thereby use it to mark off to the interests of employers a separate class of laborers.

These general considerations have a particular application to the scheme of industrial education which has been proposed for adoption by the next legislature of the state of Illinois—one of the leading industrial states of the Union, and containing its second largest city. This scheme proposes a separate State Commission of Vocational Education, and a separate Board wherever

source: *Vocational Education*, II (1913), 374–377.

the community may wish to develop any form of industrial education. In other words, the entire school system of the state as a whole and of such communities of the state as may desire to do something definite in the direction of industrial education, is split into two for the education of all above fourteen years of age. Since whatever a state like Illinois may do in such a matter is sure to have influence in other states in this formative period, educators all over the country should be aroused to help ward off what, without exaggeration, may be termed the greatest evil now threatening the interests of democracy in education.

The statement of the scheme ought to be enough to condemn it. The least reflection shows fundamentally bad features associated with it. First, it divides and duplicates the administrative educational machinery. How many communities have such an excess of public interest in education that they can afford to cut it into two parts? How many have such a surplusage of money and other resources that they can afford to maintain a double system of schools, with the waste of funds and the friction therein involved? Second, the scheme tends to paralyze one of the most vital movements now operating for the improvement of existing general education. The old time general, academic education is beginning to be vitalized by the introduction of manual, industrial, and social activities; it is beginning to recognize its responsibility to train all the youth for useful citizenship, including a calling in which each may render useful service to society and make an honest and decent living. Everywhere the existing school system is beginning to be alive to the need of supplementary agencies to help it fulfill this purpose, and is taking tentative but positive and continuous steps toward it. . . .

EVILS OF SEPARATE CONTROL
WORK BOTH WAYS

These two movements within the established American public school system, the proposed scheme, if adopted, will surely arrest. General education will be left with all its academic vices and its remoteness from the urgent realities of contemporary life untouched, and with the chief forces working for reform removed. Increasing recognition of its public and social responsibilities will be blasted. It is inconceivable that those who have loved and served our American common school system will, whatever the defects of this system, stand idly by and see such a blow aimed at it. Were anything needed to increase the force of the blow, it is the fact that the bill provides that all funds for industrial education raised by the local community be duplicated by the state, altho the funds contributed by the state for general school purposes are hardly more than five per cent of the amount raised by local taxation.

Thirdly, the segregation will work disastrously for the true interests of the pupils who attend the so-called vocational schools. Ex-Superintendent Cooley of Chicago, who is understood to be responsible for the proposed bill in its present form, has written a valuable report on "Vocational Education in Europe." He quite rightly holds in high esteem the work and opinions of Superintendent Kerschensteiner of Munich. It is noteworthy, that this leading European authority insists upon all technical and trade work being taught in its scientific and social bearings. Altho working in a country definitely based on class distinctions (and where naturally the schools are based on class lines), the one thing Superintendent Kerschensteiner has stood for has been that industrial training shall be primarily not for the sake of industries, but for the sake of citizenship, and that it be conducted therefore on a purely educational basis and not in behalf of interested manufacturers. Mr. Cooley's own report summarizes Mr. Kerschensteiner's views as follows:

If the boy is to become an efficient workman he must comprehend his work in all of its relations to science, to art, and to society in general. . . . The young workman who understands his trade in its scientific relations, its historical, economic and social bearings, will take a higher view of his trade, of his powers and duties as a citizen, and as a member of society.

Whatever may be the views of manufacturers anxious to secure the aid of the state in providing them with a somewhat better grade of laborers for them to exploit, the quotation states the point of view which is self-evident to those who approach the matter of industrial education from the side of education, and of a progressive society. It is truly extraordinary that just at a time when even partisan politics are taking a definitely progressive turn, such a reactionary measure as the institution of trade and commercial schools under separate auspices should be proposed. It is not necessary to argue concerning the personal motives of the bankers and manufacturers who have been drawn into the support of the measure. Doubtless many of them have the most public spirited intentions. But no one experienced in education can doubt what would be the actual effect of a system of schools conducted wholly separate from the regular public schools, with a totally different curriculum, and with teachers and pupils responsible to a totally independent and separate school administration. Whatever were the original motives and intentions, such schools would not and could not give their pupils a knowledge of industry or any particular occupation in relation to "science, art and society in general." To attempt this would involve duplicating existing schools, in addition to providing proper industrial training. And it is self-evident that the economical and effective way to accomplish this move is to expand and supplement the present school system. Not being able to effect this complete duplication, these new schools would be confined to aiming at increased efficiency in certain narrow lines.

UNITY OF PUBLIC SCHOOL SYSTEM ESSENTIAL

Those who believe in the continued separate existence of what they are pleased to call the "lower classes" or the "laboring classes" would naturally rejoice to have schools in which these "classes" would be segregated. And some employers of labor would doubtless rejoice to have schools supported by public taxation supply them with additional food for their mills. All others should be united against every proposition, in whatever form advanced, to separate training of employees from training for citizenship, training of intelligence and character from training for narrow industrial efficiency. That the evil forces at work are not local is seen in the attempt to get the recent national convention on industrial education in Philadelphia to commit itself in favor of the Illinois scheme. . . .

17

Vocational Education
JOHN D. RUSSELL AND ASSOCIATES
(1938)

The Russell report registered substantial criticisms of the existing federal support programs for vocational education and called for modifications in the Smith–Hughes guidelines, while simultaneously reaffirming the commitment to vocationalism in education.

A review of the favorable accomplishments of the Federal program of vocational education leaves no doubt of the fact that a considerable amount of good has resulted. In certain respects, however, it seems clear that the results of the program have been negative or unsatisfactory. . . .

Little attempt is made in this analysis to fix responsibility for the shortcomings in the program. Some of the deficiencies arise from the nature of the legislation, others may be due in part to inadequate appropriations, others may be chargeable to the administrative organization or to the personnel of the Federal executive staff, and others may be due to inadequacies in the State and local organization for vocational education. . . .

PROMOTION OF A LIMITED CONCEPT OF VOCATIONAL EDUCATION. The Federal program of vocational education has been based on the idea that instruction, to be effec-

SOURCE: Prepared for the Advisory Committee on Education, Staff Study No. 8 (Washington, D.C., 1938), pp. 125–130, 153–156, 238–240.

tive, must be very specific and narrowly related to the occupational skills it seeks to develop. . . .

The terms of the Act seem to make possible a relatively broad definition of the type of instruction that might be included in the program. Despite the possibility of this broad construction, however, the reimbursement has been limited to a type of instruction defined very narrowly and specifically, particularly in the field of trades and industries. Without denying the value of specific training under certain circumstances, many competent educators would hold that a generalized type of training may be just as valuable, particularly in a time of rapid technological change. It is entirely possible that the specific processes learned in the training period may be obsolete before the trainee has an opportunity to enter employment.

There has been vigorous promotion of the idea that vocational education and general education are two entirely distinct and separate things. The existence of the federally adopted definition of vocational education has tended to distort the whole concept of the type of instruction that is suitable as preparation for useful employment. This promotion of a very limited concept of the type of education that is suitable for occupational training must be viewed as one of the unfavorable accomplishments of the Federal program.

Not only has the general concept of vocational education been limited, but the occupational fields for which training has been provided through the Smith–Hughes and subsequent acts by no means embrace all the vocational opportunities available to American youth for which training would be valuable. It may be granted that the federal Government properly has the function of calling attention to specific fields of occupational training for which inadequate provision is being made by the States. There would at the same time be considerable advantage in leaving the States free to decide upon the types of occupations for which they wish to offer training in their schools. The Federal funds should be made available not only for occupational preparation of certain specified types, but also for preparation for any other occupations which in the judgment of State authorities is desirable.

DIVERSION OF FUNDS FROM GENERAL EDUCATION. In certain States . . . the requirements that the Federal funds be matched by State or local funds has without doubt led to a diversion of some funds to vocational education that otherwise would have been available for general education. This diversion cannot be criticized adversely if a good program of general education is being provided. In a number of States with limited economic ability, however, it seems clear that the first claim upon the available State and local funds should be for the maintenance of a sound and adequate program of general education, particularly at the elementary level. . . .

ENCOURAGEMENT OF A DUAL SYSTEM OF SCHOOLS. The American educational system is based upon the unit type of organization, whereby a single line of advancement is provided for all pupils from the kindergarten or first grade of the elementary school through the secondary school and the institution of higher education. This American plan for a school system is in distinct contrast to the European ideas of school organization, where one series of schools and one line of advancement are provided for the masses and an entirely separate series of schools and a different line of advancement for the upper classes or the elite. The unit system seems to be the only plan compatible with the ideals of American

democracy, and this concept is a fundamental charac-
teristic of the school system in the United States.

The program in vocational education has to some
extent disregarded this American ideal of a single system of schools, and has encouraged the creation of a
dual or separate school system for the education of workers. Stated in plainest terms, the concept behind the
program of vocational education would segregate the
young people who are , to become industrial workers
from those who are to go into the professions and other
scholarly pursuits, and would provide separate school
facilities for these two groups. In the case of agriculture,
it is usually necessary, because of the small school units
that are typical of rural areas, to give the vocational
courses in the regular high schools; but even in such
cases there seems to be a deliberate attempt to keep the
vocational work as separate as possible from the other
phases of the educational program.

A number of facts may be cited as evidence of deliberate planning for the separation of vocational education from general education. The requirements of the
scheduling of classes in vocational education enforce this
distinction even where the program of vocational education is given in a cosmopolitan type of school. A separate program of club activities, organized nationally
under the sponsorship of the Federal Office, is set up
for pupils in reimbursed classes in agriculture. The lines
of administrative authority, which in vocational education run more or less directly from the local teacher of
the occupational subjects to the State supervisor of such
subjects and from the State supervisor to the Federal
officials in vocational education, tend to introduce a
division that strongly smacks of a separate or dual system. In the teacher-training program there is insistence
in many States on a sharp separation of students who

will enter service in federally reimbursed classes from students who expect to enter other types of teaching. Even the major professional organization for teachers in vocational education is set up in complete independence of the organization of teachers in the regular school system. A number of State superintendents of education, in response to a direct inquiry, stated their conviction that Federal support for vocational education had tended to cause that program to develop separate and apart from other education.

That separation of the program of vocational education from general education is deliberately encouraged can scarcely be doubted. That the creation of a dual system of schools is unwise seems to be the clear teaching of the American concept of democracy. . . .

ALL-DAY SCHOOLS. There is a substantial body of evidence to the effect that in general the highly specific training in the all-day program of many vocational schools has been of little value to boys intending to enter trades and industrial occupations. Representatives both of organized labor and of industrial management are critical of the inadequate preparation for skilled trades that is given in some of the all-day schools. In other schools it seems that the program of vocational education has developed along sound lines and is satisfactory both to the employers and to the organized labor group.

In an effort to examine carefully the criticisms of the program in vocational education in trades and industries a former president of one of the large international labor unions was employed as a special consultant for this investigation. He was assisted by another person with extensive experience in the labor movement. These staff members spent considerable time interviewing labor officials and vocational educators and collecting opinions and experiences regarding the functioning of vocational education in the public schools. . . .

The findings from this study indicate widespread dissatisfaction on the part of organized labor with the Federal program of vocational education as it is operated in the all-day schools to prepare boys for entrance into trades and industries. The specific criticisms may be discussed under six headings.

1. The authorities in charge of the program of vocational education have failed to seek advice from representatives of labor on policies affecting labor interest. . . . Organized labor was vitally interested in the provision for vocational education at the time the Smith–Hughes Act was under consideration and gave strong support to its passage in 1917. Once the law was enacted, however, the program seems to have been developed without any close contact with organized labor and the enterprise was in some instances directed into channels which showed little regard for many of the public interests necessarily involved in training for industrial pursuits.

2. In many schools pupils are lured into the trade and industrial classes under the pretense that they will be given training completely equipping them as skilled mechanics or craftsmen. The inability of pupils who have completed training to meet the requirements in the skilled trades is a source of bitter disappointment to the boys, to their parents, and to employers. It is only fair to state, however, that in many of the better schools no such inducement is held out to the boys who enroll for trade classes, but they are properly apprised of the contribution that the school can make to their future careers as craftsmen.

The misconception of the function of the school in training for trade and industrial occupations, which is found in a considerable number of local programs, has led to charges that the whole program is useless. Many employers state that they prefer to employ boys who have had only a good general high school education, rather than those who have had trade courses. This preference on the part of employers, however, may frequently arise from the desire to obtain the more intelligent individuals as employees. A general high school education usually serves as a selective device to weed out those of lower intellectual ability.

3. The program of instruction has ignored the necessity for providing thorough training in social and economic studies of value to workers entering industry.

4. Vocational education in trades and industries has tended to produce a supply of labor without reference to the demands for it or the possibility of absorbing it into employment. Under such circumstances the program of vocational education may become a very disturbing element in the labor market and may even have an unfortunate effect on the level of wages in certain occupations. To a considerable extent the Federal Office is responsible for this condition, for the ultimate evaluation of the program is largely in terms of increases in enrollments. This policy has led to continual pressure from official sources on local schools to increase the number of pupils in the trade preparatory classes. As a result, there is a tendency to admit pupils to the trade and industrial classes without regard for the needs of the community for trained craftsmen. In many cases it seems that the boys' natural love of machinery is played upon and many are induced to enter a fascinating form of school work without regard to their opportunities for employment in such vocations.

5. In many cases there has been a disregard of sound labor standards in setting up the programs of vocational

training. This has been notorious in the case of so-called plant training, in which, by arrangement with an industrial concern, preparation for employment has been given directly in the factory and the foreman paid as a teacher of a vocational subject. Beginning workers in the plant have been classified as "pupils" long after they have mastered the fundamentals of the process, and have been paid only low wages or no wages at all for a long period of time even though they were engaged in regular production. Another type of program, the cooperative plan, in which pupils spend about half their time in school and half in employment, has also been used in some cases as a device to exploit the pupils and may have had the effect locally of depressing general wage levels in certain types of work. . . .

6. There is a general opinion among the labor group that the class work in vocational education has been persistently colored by an anti-union habit of thought. Considerable support has been lent to this opinion by the recent effort to organize on a national basis the boys enrolled in trade and industrial classes. This organization, known as the Future Craftsmen of America, was launched under the sponsorship of industrial concerns and seems to be taking on characteristics that are very objectionable from the point of view of organized labor. It is most unfortunate that those in charge of the program of vocational education have allowed and encouraged developments which seem to support the contention that the program has been permitted to become a definite agency for antiunionism. Not all of the development in this direction has been deliberate. Perhaps its roots are as much in ignorance of labor objectives as in conscious opposition to them, but it has all contributed to the dissatisfaction of the labor movement with the program of vocational education in the public schools.

These indictments from the point of view of organized labor represent a serious criticism of the management of the program of vocational education in trades
and industries. The situation in the all-day schools has
shaken severely the faith which labor has traditionally
placed in the sincerity and integrity of educators. . . .

The Needs for Vocational Education

22. The best interests of society demand that every
individual be equipped for some occupation so that he
may contribute effectively to the satisfaction of human
wants. The public school has proved to be an effective
agency for occupational preparation. Much of the preparation, however, must in any case be given on the job
rather than in the school. Apprenticeship should be encouraged as a method of vocational education. . . .

25. Vocational education should immediately precede
entrance upon the occupation. Under modern conditions
this principle precludes the offering of specialized vocational courses in the junior high school period, although
exploratory courses may well be provided in the junior
high school. Much of vocational education should be
restricted to the later years of the secondary school and
the junior college. Arrangements must be made for the
vocational education of pupils of all levels of ability
above the minimum required for self-support. A special
problem is the provision of vocational education for
young people in rural areas who will later migrate to
cities.

26. Six principles are suggested for selecting the occupations for which training of a pre-entry type should
be offered in the schools: (a) A certain amount of intellectual content should be involved; (b) the training
should have general applicability to a variety of occupa-

tions; (c) employment should be available on the completion of training; (d) the time allowed should be sufficient for attaining a satisfactory degree of competence; (e) the occupation should be socially desirable; (f) the number of pupils should be sufficient to permit an economical grouping for instructional purposes. On the basis of these criteria the following occupational fields seem to be desirable for inclusion in the school program: (a) Agriculture; (b) homemaking; (c) certain phases of trades and industries; (d) office occupations; (e) distributive occupations. On an experimental basis some of the specialized public service occupations might be considered for inclusion in the school program.

27. The service of the schools in supplying vocational education for occupations of the trade and industrial type should be chiefly to cultivate in the pupils a broad range of basic abilities of value in a whole related family of occupations. The training that is given in vocational education should include instruction with reference to the social and economic situation into which the worker must fit and the legal provisions governing his employment.

28. A sound program of vocational education must include not only training, but guidance and placement. Schools furnishing vocational education should provide adequately for the guidance of pupils, and should cooperate closely with public employment offices in the initial placement and adjustment of those leaving the full-time school.

29. Data now available do not permit an accurate estimate of the total amount of funds needed for a sound and complete program of vocational education. It seems clear, however, that the amount now provided is far from sufficient to maintain a suitable program.

30. The Federal Government must take a vital inter-

est in the development of sound programs of vocational preparation. The Federal Government is justified not only in furnishing temporary stimulation to such development in the public schools, but also in undertaking the actual support of vocational education on an extensive basis. Increased Federal funds for the support of vocational education cannot be effectively utilized without a relaxation of the existing Federal restrictions on the program.

31. Federal appropriations for vocational education should not be increased until there has been a relatively generous provision of funds for general education. The greatest advances in vocational education in the long run will come through relatively large Federal grants for general, unrestricted educational purposes rather than through grants specifically limited to vocational subjects. Designation of grants for vocational education could well be discontinued as soon as there is an adequate Federal appropriation for general, unspecified educational purposes. If designation of funds for vocational education is continued, the legislation should define this type of service broadly. Guidance and co-operative placement services should be included, and instruction at the junior college and adult levels should be particularly encouraged.

18

Life Adjustment Education

COMMISSION ON LIFE ADJUSTMENT EDUCATION

OF YOUTH

(1951)

The life adjustment movement called for a reordering of secondary education toward more practical concerns.

The goal of the Commission is to assist in increasing the effectiveness of present efforts through education to meet the imperative needs of all youth. To that end it is concerned with stimulating programs which more adequately meet the needs of pupils now in school. Even more, it is concerned with the types of education needed by the adolescent youth who drop out of school because their needs are not being met realistically. . . .

The question may well be raised, Why should another effort be made at this time to effect major improvements in secondary education when so many significant attempts have already been made or are now in progress? The most obvious answer is that despite the significant progress made to this end during recent years, there is still so much to be done. American high schools do not attract and hold many boys and girls long enough to meet their life needs . . . over the country approximately eighty per cent of youth enter the ninth grade; approximately forty per cent remain to be graduated from high schools. . . .

SOURCE: U.S. Office of Education, *Life Adjustment Education for Every Youth*, Bulletin No. 22, 1951, pp. 7–8, 12–13.

Two things are essential to meet the educational needs of all American youth. They are (1) a recognition by the general public of the inadequacies of the means existing for meeting youth problems, and (2) a determination by the faculty of each school that it will do its best with the resources which are available to meet the needs of all youth in the community. In the last analysis secondary education will be improved by teachers, parents, and civic leaders working together in local schools and communities. The Commission on Life Adjustment Education for Youth can and will perform the function of stimulating action, coordinating efforts, encouraging promising innovations, and bringing the issues more prominently to the attention of teachers and the general public.

19
Slums and Suburbs
JAMES B. CONANT
(1961)

This explicit plea to integrate schooling with the employment needs of America's urban black youth by the former president of Harvard University aroused considerable interest and controversy.

In a slum section composed almost entirely of Negroes in one of our largest cities the following situation was found: A total of fifty-nine per cent of the male youth between the ages of sixteen and twenty-one were out of school and unemployed. They were roaming the streets. Of the boys who graduated from high school forty-eight per cent were unemployed in contrast to sixty-three per cent of the boys who had dropped out of school. In short, two thirds of the male dropouts did not have jobs and about half of the high school graduates did not have jobs. In such a situation, the pupil may ask, "Why bother to stay in school when graduation for half the boys opens onto a dead-end street?" . . .

At the outset I must record an educational heresy, or rather support a proposition that many will accept as self-evident but that some professors of the liberal arts will denounce as dangerously heretical. *I submit that in a heavily urbanized and industrialized free society the educational experiences of youth should fit their subsequent employment.* There should be a smooth transi-

SOURCE: *Slums and Suburbs* (New York, 1961), pp. 33–34, 40–41.

tion from full-time schooling to a full-time job, whether that transition be after grade ten or after graduation from high school, college, or university. . . .

Although half or more of the graduates of many high schools seek employment immediately on graduation, only in a few cities does one find an effective placement service. I make this statement without intending any reproach to either social agencies, employment offices, or to guidance officers. The obligations of the school should not end when the student either drops out of school or graduates. At that point the cumulative record folder concerning a student's educational career is usually brought to an end. It should not be. To my mind, *guidance officers, especially in the large cities, ought to be given the responsibility for following the post-high school careers of youth from the time they leave school until they are twenty-one years of age.* Since compulsory attendance usually ends at age sixteen, this means responsibility for the guidance of youth ages sixteen to twenty-one who are out of school and either employed or unemployed. This expansion of the school's function will cost money and will mean additional staff—at least a doubling of the guidance staff in most of the large cities. But the expense is necessary, for vocational and educational guidance must be a continuing process to help assure a smooth transition from school to the world of work. The present abrupt break between the two is unfortunate. What I have in mind suggests, of course, a much closer relationship than now exists among the schools, employers, and labor unions, as well as social agencies and employment offices.

20

The Bridge between Man and His Work

ADVISORY COUNCIL ON VOCATIONAL EDUCATION

(1968)

This report laid the basis for the 1968 amendments to the Vocational Education Act of 1963. Its focus was the enlargement of the concept of vocational training and the necessity to integrate more effectively the poor, unemployed, and underemployed into the economic system.

IV. BASIC CONCEPTS OF EDUCATION FOR EMPLOYMENT

. . . The Vocational Education Act of 1963 in many ways charted a major reorientation of vocational education. However, in the brief time available, the promise of the act has not been realized. Meantime the world of work and the problems of preparation for it, access to it, and successful performance in it have become even more complex. Out of the changing social and economic environment of the past two decades has emerged clearer concepts of career development, some new and some modifications of earlier ones. From these concepts we can draw operational principles and design a system of legislative and administrative changes necessary for achieving vocational education for all. Three concepts are particularly relevant to this report.

SOURCE: Ninetieth Congress, Second Session, U.S. Senate, *Notes and Working Papers Concerning the Administration of Programs Authorized Under Vocational Education Act of 1963 Public Law 88-210 as Amended,* Prepared for the Subcommittee on Education of the Committee on Labor and Public Welfare (1968), pp. 47-52.

ACADEMIC AND VOCATIONAL EDUCATION

It is no longer possible to compartmentalize education into general, academic, and vocational components. Education is a crucial element in preparation for a successful working career at any level. With rising average educational attainment, better educated people are available so that the employer seldom needs to accept the less educated. If it represents nothing else, a high school diploma is evidence of consistency, persistence, some degree of self-discipline, and perhaps even of docility. The relevance of education for employment arises from better educated labor and a technology that requires it. The educational skills of spoken and written communication, computation, analytical techniques, knowledge of society and one's role in it, and skill in human relations are as vital as the skills of particular occupations.

On the other hand, employability skills are equally essential to education. If education is preparation for life, and if practically everyone's life and opportunities for self-expression and self-fulfillment include work, then only the successfully employable are successfully educated. American society is achievement oriented and attributes something less than wholeness to the nonstriver and nonachiever. Culture and vocation are inseparable and unseverable aspects of humanity.

Vocational education is not a separate discipline within education, but it is a basic objective of all education and must be a basic element of each person's education. It is also a teaching technique which may have even more to offer as method than as substance. As a selecting out process for the professions, education has fostered, stressed, and rewarded the verbal skills important to these pursuits. It has given too little attention to development of attitudes, manipulative skills, and adaptability to new situations. In the process of emphasizing verbal skills, the predominant methods of instruction are lecture and discussion, and little attention is given to the alternative technique of learning by doing. . . . For many students, the techniques of vocational education can supply a core around which an attractive package of academic as well as skill content can be prepared which will be more palatable and useful to undermotivated students than either alone. This may be most applicable to those from deprived environments whose verbal experiences have been limited and whose time horizons have been shortened by expectation of failure. Skill development can be accomplished through work experience or through education in the school's shops and laboratories. The key is to build a better means of integrating academic education, skill training, and work experience. The common objective should be a successful life in which employment has a crucial role.

THE CONSTANCY OF CHANGE

The second premise is by now a cliche: "Nothing will henceforth be more constant than change." Technological and economic progress feeds on itself, opening new vistas and closing the old. The underprepared are threatened by displacement, and the well prepared are confronted with new opportunities. Both require adaptability. Preventive measures can reduce the demand for remedial programs but never eliminate the need for them. Appropriately prepared persons may be highly adaptable, but that adaptability may depend upon upgrading present skills as well as acquiring new ones. The need for continuous learning, formal or informal, will certainly become universal. There will always be those with inadequate preventive occupational preparation who will need remedial help.

The demand upon vocational education is clear: Programs for youth must prepare them for change; programs for adults must be universally available, and must emphasize coping with change.

TOWARD FREEDOM OF OPPORTUNITY

Finally, the most treasured value of our society is the worth and freedom of the individual. Each individual is entitled to the benefits of a social system which will make it possible for him to get from where he is to where he has the potential to be. One operational measure of freedom is the range of choice available to the individual. The major constraints upon the range of choice are ignorance and poverty and disease and discrimination. Education can reduce the barriers of ignorance and proper occupational preparation can lower the barriers of poverty. They cannot eliminate disease and discrimination but they can substantially contribute to overcoming them.

A number of operational principles follow from these premises:

1. Vocational education cannot be meaningfully limited to the skills necessary for a particular occupation. It is more appropriately defined as all of those aspects of educational experience which help a person to discover his talents, to relate them to the world of work, to choose an occupation, and to refine his talents and use them successfully in employment. In fact, orientation and assistance in vocational choice may often be more valid determinants of employment success, and

therefore more profitable uses of educational funds, than specific skill training.

2. In a technology where only relative economic costs, not engineering know-how, prevent mechanization of routine tasks, the age of "human use of human beings" may be within reach, but those human beings must be equipped to do tasks which machines cannot do. Where complex instructions and sophisticated decisions mark the boundary between the realm of man and the role of the machine, there is no longer room for any dichotomy between intellectual competence and manipulative skills and, therefore, between academic and vocational education.

3. In a labor force where most have a high school education, all who do not are at a serious competitive disadvantage. But at the same time, a high school education alone cannot provide an automatic ticket to satisfactory and continuous employment. Education cannot shed its responsibilities to the student (and to society in his behalf) just because he has chosen to reject the system or because it has handed him a diploma. In a world where the distance between the experiences of childhood, adolescence, and adulthood and between school and work continually widen, the school must reach forward to assist the student across the gaps just as labor market institutions must reach back to assist in the transition. It is not enough to dump the school leaver into a labor market pool. The school along with the rest of society must provide him a ladder, and perhaps help him to climb it.

4. Some type of formal occupational preparation must be a part of every educational experience. Though it may be well to delay final occupational choice until all the alternatives are known, no one ought to leave the educational system without a salable skill. In addition,

given the rapidity of change and the competition from generally rising educational attainment, upgrading and remedial education opportunities are a continual necessity. Those who need occupational preparation most, both preventive and remedial, will be those least prepared to take advantage of it and most difficult to educate and train. Yet for them, particularly, equal rights do not mean equal opportunity. Far more important is the demonstration of equal results.

5. The objective of vocational education should be the development of the individual, not the needs of the labor market. One of the functions of an economic system is to structure incentives in such a way that individuals will freely choose to accomplish the tasks which need to be done. Preparation for employment should be flexible and capable of adapting the system to the individual's need rather than the reverse. The system for occupational preparation should supply a salable skill at any terminal point chosen by the individual, yet no doors should be closed to future progress and development.

In short, an environment is emerging in which nearly all require salable skills which demand intellectual as well as manipulative content and which include the base for constant adaptation to change. An increasing amount of the knowledge necessary to success must be organized and presented in a formal manner; the pickup or observation methods of the past are no longer adequate. Rural schools with their inadequate offerings and ghetto schools with their deficient resources, added to the initial environmental handicaps of their students, can never hope, without special assistance, to gain on the quality-conscious suburban schools. Education is neither the unique cause, nor the sole cure of the problems of the rural depressed area or the urban slum. But it is a necessary factor.

V. Toward a Unified System of Vocational Education

That most of the concepts of section IV were in the minds of the authors of the Vocational Education Act of 1963 is apparent from its declaration of purpose "that persons of all ages in all communities of the State—those in high school, those who have completed or discontinued their formal education and are preparing to enter the labor market, those who have already entered the labor market but need to upgrade their skills or learn new ones, and those with special educational handicaps —will have ready access to vocational training or retraining which is of high quality, which is realistic in the light of actual or anticipated opportunities for gainful employment, and which is suited to their needs, interests, and ability to benefit from such training."

An adequate system of vocational education capable of achieving these objectives while coping with a changing environment should, we believe, have the following characteristics:

1. Occupational preparation should begin in the elementary schools with a realistic picture of the world of work. Its fundamental purposes should be to familiarize the student with his world and to provide him with the intellectual tools and rational habits of thought to play a satisfying role in it.

2. In junior high school economic orientation and occupational preparation should reach a more sophisticated stage with study by all students of the economic and industrial system by which goods and services are produced and distributed. The objective should be ex-

posure to the full range of occupational choices which
will be available at a later point and full knowledge of
the relative advantages and the requirements of each.

3. Occupational preparation should become more specific in the high school, though preparation should not
be limited to a specific occupation. Given the uncertain-
ties of a changing economy and the limited experiences
upon which vocational choices must be made, instruction should not be overly narrow but should be built
around significant families of occupations or industries
which promise expanding opportunities.

All students outside the college preparatory curriculum should acquire an entry-level job skill, but they
should also be prepared for post-high-school vocational
and technical education. Even those in the college preparatory curriculum might profit from the techniques of
learning by doing. On the other hand, care should be
taken that pursuit of a vocationally oriented curriculum
in the high school does not block the upward progress
of the competent student who later decides to pursue a
college degree.

4. Occupational education should be based on a spiral
curriculum which treats concepts at higher and higher
levels of complexity as the student moves through the
program. Vocational preparation should be used to
make general education concrete and understandable;
general education should point up the vocational implications of all education. Curriculum materials should
be prepared for both general and vocational education
to emphasize these relationships.

5. Some formal postsecondary occupational preparation for all should be a goal for the near future. Universal high school education is not yet achieved but is rapidly approaching reality. Postsecondary enrollments are
growing, and before many years have passed, the labor

force entrant without advanced skills gained through postsecondary education, apprenticeship, or on-the-job training will be at a serious disadvantage. Universal advanced training will bring increased productivity, higher standards of living, and greater adaptability, to the profit of the economy as well as the individual. If postsecondary education and training is to be universal, it must be free. Fourteen years of free public education with a terminal occupational emphasis should be a current goal.

6. Beyond initial preparation for employment, many, out of choice or necessity, will want to bolster an upward occupational climb with part-time and sometimes full-time, courses and programs as adults. These should be available as part of the regular public school system. They should not be limited to a few high-demand and low-cost trades, but should provide a range of occupational choice as wide as those available to students preparing for initial entry.

7. Any occupation which contributes to the good of society is a fit subject for vocational education. In the allocation of scarce resources, first attention must be paid to those occupations which offer expanding opportunities for employment. In the elementary and junior high school, attention can be paid only to groups of occupations which employ large numbers of people, and instruction must be restricted to broad principles, common skills, and pervasive attitudes which will be useful in a broad range of employment. These restrictions are less and less valid as the student goes through high school and junior college, until, in adult education, instruction is justified in even the most restricted field if it is valuable to the individual and to society.

8. Occupational preparation need not and should not be limited to the classroom, to the school shop, or to the

laboratory. Many arguments favor training on the job. Expensive equipment need not be duplicated. Familiarization with the environment and discipline of the workplace is an important part of occupational preparation, yet is difficult to simulate in a classroom. Supervisors and other employees can double as instructors. The trainee learns by earning. On the other hand, the employer and his supervisors may be more production than training oriented. The operations and equipment of a particular employer may cover only part of a needed range of skills, necessitating transfer among employers for adequate training. The ideal is to meld the advantages of institutional and on-the-job training in formal cooperative work-study programs.

9. Effective occupational preparation is impossible if the school feels that its obligation ends when the student graduates. The school, therefore, must work with employers to build a bridge between school and work. Placing the student on a job and following up his successes and failures provides the best possible information to the school on its own strengths and weaknesses.

10. No matter how good the system of initial preparation and the opportunities for upgrading on the job, there will always be need for remedial programs. Remedial programs will differ from the preventive in that many of the students will require financial assistance while in training; the courses must be closely oriented to the labor market to assure a quick return to employment; and the trainee will be impatient of what may seem to be the frills of regular vocational programs.

11. At every level from the elementary school through the postsecondary, adult, and remedial programs there will be those with special needs as defined by the 1963 act. For both humanitarian and economic reasons, persons with special needs deserve special help.

12. Many communities are too small to muster sufficient students for a range of occupational offerings broad enough to provide realistic freedom of occupational choice. Potential students, often those with the greatest needs, live in areas too isolated for access to meaningful training. Others come from a home and neighborhood environment which makes sound preparation for life and employment difficult. An adequate system of occupational preparation will provide residential facilities wherever their absence presents an obstacle to anyone in need of education and training.

13. The public system for occupational preparation must be supported by adequate facilities and equipment, buttressed by research and innovation, and by the preparation and upgrading of competent teachers, counselors, and administrators. To assure constant improvement, it must provide for constant evaluation and reporting of problems and accomplishments.

14. The system of occupational preparation cannot operate in a vacuum. Data must be made available on public and private training opportunities to eliminate undesirable duplication. Data on supply and demand for various occupations must be available on a broader and more accurate basis. But total training opportunities must be based, not on the number of jobs which are available, but on the number of persons needing training.

Creation of the system of occupational preparation outlined here must be a continuing pursuit. The Vocational Education Act of 1963 and the efforts of vocational educators have carried the Nation a substantial way toward these objectives. Our recommendations which follow will, if adopted, assure further progress. But they will never end the quest because, fortunately, society does not stand still.

21

Career Education
SIDNEY P. MARLAND, JR.

A recent proposal to make vocational education more flexible and more comprehensive is here offered in an interview with the former U.S. Commissioner of Education.

[Question:] Commissioner Marland, on several occasions recently you have talked of "career education." What is the difference between career education and vocational education?

[Marland:] Speaking just in terms of the schools, career education—as I see it—would embrace vocational education but would go a good deal further. I suppose all of us are familiar with the situation of a young person finishing high school or even college with no idea of what kind of work he would like to follow. This is a depressing proposition for the student and in my view a failure on the part of the schools. So what I would hope for is a new orientation of education—starting with the earliest grades and continuing through high school—that would expose the student to the range of career opportunities, help him narrow down the choices in terms of his own aptitudes and interests, and provide him with education and training appropriate to his ambition. In many cases his training would certainly involve the "manipulative" skills commonly associated with vocational education.

SOURCE: *American Education,* VII (November, 1971), pp. 25–26.

It would be strongly and relevantly undergirded by education in the traditional academic subjects.

In any event, what the term "career education" means to me is basically a point of view, a concept—a concept that says three things: First, that career education will be part of the curriculum for all students, not just some. Second, that it will continue throughout a youngster's stay in school, from the first grade through senior high and beyond, if he so elects. And third, that every student leaving school will possess the skills necessary to give him a start in making a livelihood for himself and his family, even if he leaves before completing high school. . . .

[Question:] How might career education work out in a given school system?

[Marland:] Responding just for the purposes of illustration, I would say that there would probably be two basic aspects to the approach in a given school district. The first would have to do with the proposition that experts have identified some twenty thousand different kinds of jobs. Obviously, that is far too great a number for any individual to comprehend. However, those jobs can be grouped within general clusters. Some examples from one suggested arrangement are Business and Office Occupations, Marketing and Distribution Occupations, Communication and Media Occupations, Manufacturing Occupations, and Fine Arts and Humanities Occupations.

During the first six years of his schooling the youngster would be made familiar with these various clusters of occupations and what is involved in entering them. In grades seven and eight he would concentrate on learning more about those particular job clusters that interest him most. In grades nine and ten he would select a job cluster to explore in some depth, an experience that would include visiting places where this kind of work is going on, trying his own hand at certain basic skills, and in general getting practical experience in what that line of work involves. In grades eleven and twelve he would pursue his selected job area even more intensely, in terms of one of three options: acquiring skills that would enable him to take a job immediately upon leaving high school; taking a combination of academic and on-the-job courses in preparation for entering a post-secondary institution that would train him as a technician, for instance; or electing a somewhat similar combination of courses in preparation for a professional degree from a four-year college and beyond.

That is the curriculum aspect of the career education concept. Hand in glove with it would go a refocusing of classes in the basic subject areas—math, science, language arts, and social studies—in such a way that these classes were presented in terms of the student's career interests. One of the major benefits of this kind of refocusing would be that school would immediately become more relevant. The student would not be learning just for learning's sake or because someone ordered him to, but because the subjects he was studying would bear directly and specifically on his planned career. We feel this has particular usefulness in motivating the student who is now less than successful in school.

Marvin Lazerson is an Associate Professor of Education at the University of British Columbia. He received his doctorate in American history from Harvard University in 1970 and taught at the Harvard Graduate School of Education between 1969 and 1972. The author of *Origins of the Urban School: Public Education in Massachusetts, 1870–1915* (1971), he has also published articles and reviews in the *History of Education Quarterly, Harvard Educational Review,* and *Urban Education.* The recipient of fellowships from the Harvard-M.I.T. Joint Center for Urban Studies and the Social Science Research Council, his primary interests include urban educational history and the history of early childhood education.

W. Norton Grubb is currently a research economist with the Childhood and Government Project, University of California at Berkeley. He received his undergraduate degree in economics at Harvard in 1969, and is currently completing the Ph.D. requirements, again in the Harvard Department of Economics. He is the co-author of the forthcoming *States and Schools: The Political Economy of School Resource Inequalities.*

American Education and Vocationalism

A DOCUMENTARY HISTORY
1870-1970

CLASSICS IN EDUCATION
Lawrence A. Cremin, General Editor

The Classics in Education series presents the sources of our educational heritage. Many of the volumes combine selections from important documents with readable, up-to-date discussion of their place in the history of educational thought and their bearing on recent theory and practice. Others are reprints of monographs that have significantly affected contemporary historical interpretation. All of the Classics offer fresh perspective on current educational policy.

TEACHERS COLLEGE PRESS
TEACHERS COLLEGE, COLUMBIA UNIVERSITY